PRAISE F

"Mary truly is amazing! Thanks to her, I have learned so much about writing. She made me laugh. She made me cry. She made me a better writer!"

M. CHURCHILL

"I've read many books on the craft of writing, and *Writing Irresistible Kidlit* is among the best. I've never been so excited to get to the keyboard."

ALAN HARELL

"After writing a novel, unpublished writers inhabit an unguided middle space between not being important enough to warrant industry attention, and needing professional feedback to see how they stack up in the market. That is where Mary Kole lives. Her advice is sound, she pulls no punches, and if you listen to her, your work will improve."

ANDRES FAZA

"I would highly recommend learning from Mary Kole to anyone seriously looking to improve their writing."

KATE K.

"Mary is a top professional in the industry and her advice is on-point and actionable. Having Mary on your team will no doubt improve your pitch, manuscript, query, or whatever you're writing."

ELANA I.

"From now on, if I see a writing craft book with Mary Kole's name on it, I will hit the 'one click purchase' button without a second thought. She respects writers. She feels for writers. She understands writers. She knows exactly what insights writers need as they work. *Writing Irresistible Kidlit* is possibly the very best book on writing craft I have read in twenty-five years."

SPROCKET

"Mary Kole made me feel a renewed enthusiasm towards my writing goals."

SUSAN

"*Writing Irresistible Kidlit* is quite simply, the best 'how to' book on novel writing that I've ever read and probably ever will read in my life."

CAROL

"Mary Kole helped me to find my way. Her suggestions on my query letter are just what I needed to begin fearlessly searching for a place to call my own. I now consider Mary Kole my secret weapon."

TRACY

SUCCESSFUL QUERY LETTERS

40+ REAL WORLD QUERY LETTERS WITH LITERARY AGENT FEEDBACK

MARY KOLE

GOOD STORY PUBLISHING

"Successful Query Letters"
By Mary Kole

FIRST EDITION
1. Reference / Writing, Research, and Publishing Guides / Writing

Ebook ISBN: 978-1-939162-02-1
Print ISBN: 978-1-939162-03-8

Cover Design: Jenna Van Rooy
Editing: Amy Wilson
Printed in the United States of America

For Theo, Finn, and Ella—with all the love in the world.

CONTENTS

ABOUT THE AUTHOR

A former literary agent, Mary Kole knows the ins and outs of the publishing industry. But her favorite part has always been working directly with writers, so she founded Mary Kole Editorial in 2013 to provide consulting and developmental editing services to clients across all categories and genres. She started Good Story Company in 2019, with the aim of creating valuable content, like the Good Story Podcast, Good Story YouTube channel, and Good Story Learning membership community.

Her Story Mastermind small group workshop intensives help writers level up their craft, she offers done-for-you revision and ghostwriting for Manuscript Studio, and marketing services with Good Story Marketing. She also develops unique and commercial intellectual property for middle grade, young adult, and adult readers with Upswell Media and Bittersweet Books.

She's appeared at regional, national, and international writing conferences for the SCBWI, Writer's Digest, Penn Writers, Writer's League of Texas, San Francisco Writers Conference, WIFYR, Writing Day, and many others.

Her guest lectures have taken her to Harvard, the Ringling College of Art and Design, the Highlights Foundation, and more. Mary's recorded video classes can be found online at Writing Mastery Academy, Writing Blueprints, Udemy, and LinkedIn Learning.

Mary holds an MFA in Creative Writing and began her publishing career with a literary agency internship and the Kidlit blog, which she started in 2009. She has worked at Chronicle Books, the Andrea Brown Literary Agency, and Movable Type Management. Her books are *Writing Irresistible Kidlit: The Ultimate Guide to Crafting Fiction for Young Adult and Middle Grade Readers* from Writer's Digest Books/Penguin Random House, and *Successful Query Letters, Writing Irresistible Picture Books,* and *How to Write a Book Now* from Good Story Publishing.

Originally from the San Francisco Bay Area, she now lives with her three children, husband, two pugs, and a cat, in Minneapolis, MN.

MARY KOLE

"Receiving Mary's feedback on my novel has been one of the best things that has happened to my writing in recent years. Thanks to her, I see the possibilities in my book and also feel like a fire has been lit under me to continue. I know the work is not yet done, but today—*today*—I feel like it's possible."

ANONYMOUS

---

facebook.com / goodstoryco
x.com / goodstoryco
instagram.com / goodstorycompany
linkedin.com / company / goodstorycompany
pinterest.com / goodstorycompany
tiktok.com / @goodstoryco
youtube.com / goodstory

Query Letter Introduction

INTRODUCTION

The query letter looms large in the writerly imagination. It always has. When I was a literary agent on the conference circuit—sometimes doing two or three large speaking events a month—I would marvel that nine out of ten questions from attendees in the audience seemed to be about *that dang query letter*. Not about the finer points of the writing craft. Not about publishing and career considerations. The trend was so pronounced that my fellow agents and I would laugh about it at the happy hours.

This always seemed a bit shortsighted, but I understood why. To a writer hoping to break into print, the query letter seems like a powerful foot in the door. It's also much easier to control (and obsess over!) a one-page document, instead of a head-spinning three-hundred-page novel.

Queries are also mysterious. Most writers don't have a slush pile at their disposal, and rarely get the opportunity to glimpse what their peers are doing. Querying writers tend to keep their letters close to the vest due to superstition or self-doubt, especially as they approach submission with their projects. (Some also worry about idea theft, though these concerns are largely unfounded.)

If writers get meaningful feedback on their queries or manuscripts, they generally don't share this with peers outside of a writing group or workshop.

How are most writers, then, supposed to level up their query craft when they don't see many queries other than their own? When they don't get a chance to hear agent and publisher feedback on this important component of the submission package?

Enter this resource. Here, I've collected forty-three real, live query letters from real, live writers who have agreed to have their letters analyzed. There are queries across various categories and genres (fiction, nonfiction, children's book, etc.). Some have received offers of literary representation and book deals. Some need work. Not only will you read the query itself and learn how other writers are crafting their pitches, but you will get a former literary agent's honest and constructive response to each.

The purpose of this guide is to give you all the tools you need to confidently approach your own cover letter. Yes, that's right. The query is just a glorified cover letter, at the end of the day. When I was agenting, I would never offer representation based on the query alone. That's important to remember. The manuscript always, always came first.

Let's dive in with an overview of the query letter in general terms, as well as a breakdown of the submission process. After that, we'll get to the heart of this book—the individual queries themselves!

Bonus Tip: You'll see links and other resources cited in this guide. All of these links are clickable and will take you to articles, other chapters in this guide, and specific book titles. All of the articles and additional resources referenced herein are also collected in the Articles and Resources chapter.)

QUERY LETTER COMPONENTS

The query letter tends to confuse and confound writers because there are several ingredients and many options for arranging them. You will see the query's parts at work, in various configurations and iterations, in the examples. But let's define our query letter components here so we're all (bad publishing joke incoming) on the same page.

Personalization

If you have a specific personal reason for contacting the agent or publisher, mention it. For example, "I'm querying you because you represented my favorite book, *Title*." This speaks to that agent or publisher's experience.

If you want to remind the gatekeeper of a previous interaction, that's always relevant, too. For example, "I'm querying you because we met at (Name of Writing Conference in Month, Year), and you requested the first ten pages of my work." If you have it, use it!

An example of bad personalization would be, "I'm querying you because of your passion for literature." This is vague and can be said of anyone working in the book business. Agents and publishers, of all people, can recognize a form letter. So if this is the best you have to offer, omit the personalization element. This section is optional.

Your best weapon here is strong research to find connection points with the people you're querying, if at all possible. (A word of warning here: Depending on how deeply you dive into ~~stalking~~ learning about various gatekeepers, which is discussed in the Agent and Publisher Research Resources chapter, you may find personal information, like a person's individual social media, children's names, etc. Only use these details if you are *sure* you're hitting an appropriate tone. The more personal you get, the easier it is to come off as downright creepy.)

Comparative Titles

If you find that you have something in common with books or authors already on shelves, feel free to use comp titles to bolster your pitch. For more considerations on choosing comps, check out these articles:

"Finding Comp Titles"

"Comparative Titles in a Query"

It's important to remember that the comp title section is optional, especially if you don't have anything compelling to put here.

Many writers seem to be increasingly convinced that comparative titles are some kind of secret code that will unlock a manuscript request. Not true, but they're nice to use if you have good ones.

The Logline

A logline can rely on your comps ("It's *Sharknado* meets *Water for Elephants*") or you can write a one-or-two sentence pitch (maximum!) that summarizes your story. Another approach is to write two sentences that emphasize your character's driving narrative arc and the heart of the plot. For example, "A girl must fight a group of teenagers to the death to save her own sister and redeem her country." (This is *The Hunger Games.*) Don't skimp on the high drama of your story. The logline is where it should come out to play.

If you are already using personalization and comp titles, you can skip the logline. Remember that loglines are largely optional, because you are going to be pitching the story in much more detail with your query meat. However, some writers really like to start with a punchy sentence or two right away. This is a stylistic choice.

Manuscript Logistics

This is where you mention the title, genre, category, word count, and anything else relevant to your manuscript, like any unusual narrative choices. For example, "*Title* is a 51,000-word middle grade fantasy manuscript told in second person direct address," or, "Told in dual narrative POV, *Title* is a 75,000-word literary novel in verse." The title, word count, and target audience are the bare minimum here. ("*Title* is a 450-word picture book.")

You'll notice that I am using the terms "category" and "genre" separately, which might be a bit confusing. This terminology is very intentional. "Category" refers to target audience, for example, "the chapter book category." This is especially relevant in children's book publishing, where there are many different categories or target audiences. "Genre" refers instead to content, for example, "the fantasy genre."

It would be incorrect to call "picture book" a genre. It is a category. This small tweak can help you sound more professional in your pitch.

Query Meat

The heart of the query is the query meat, and I unpack it in more detail in the following Writing the Query Meat chapter. It pertains specifically to fiction and memoir projects, and really helps you make a case for engaging gatekeepers.

It should be between one and three paragraphs long, and will present the character and plot of your fiction or memoir project. For nonfiction, it identifies or creates a sense of market need for your specific slant on a topic. For picture books and book proposals, which will usually be enclosed after the pitch in their entirety, the query meat can be shorter.

Picture books will focus on character, plot, and the universal theme or lesson learned. Book proposal queries (which are more cover letters than anything) will focus on market, the unique selling proposition of the project, and the writer's marketing reach.

Bio Paragraph

This section is all about you. It's strange when this component is entirely missing, so think of at least one sentence to include. On the other hand, don't go overboard with voice, jokes, or personality. Don't make your bio longer than the query meat. Include only professional-sounding and relevant details. If you have writing credits, publications, or competition wins or placements, make sure to cite specifics (publisher and year, for example). Otherwise, gatekeepers will assume that you self-published your previous work or entered contests where everyone who pays the fee gets a prize. If this is the case, say so. There really is no shame about these choices, but hiding parts of your resume or spinning the truth might land you in trouble.

Finally, avoid being too cheeky in this section. The number of cats you have is probably not going to be relevant, unless you are writing a cat book. Focus on your literary education (if any), publishing credentials (if any), and life experience that's related to the project at hand.

Query Logistics

This is your breezy sign-off . It can literally be the following:

> "Per your submission guidelines, the first (# of pages or chapters) are pasted below. Please note that this is a simultaneous submission. Thank you very much for your time and consideration."

If you don't know what a simultaneous submission is, see the Submission Strategy chapter for a short discussion on this important issue.

Signature

The final component of your query letter is exactly what it sounds like. Your real name, a pen name (if you're using one), your contact information (ideally email and phone number, at minimum, but you can include your mailing address), and then any online credentials like your website URL and social media profiles. These can all go underneath the letter on separate lines.

In the example queries, this portion will appear as (Signature), as most of our contributors have requested some level of anonymity.

Your writing sample, if you're sending one, will follow. Please see the Manuscript Formatting and Illustrations chapter for more. But first, let's really dig into that all-important query meat.

WRITING THE QUERY MEAT

Whether you pitch an agent in person or with a written query, your goal is the same: to get the gatekeeper to request your manuscript. And you can usually do that by framing your story in a way that makes them care.

If you answer the following questions about your fiction or memoir[1] manuscript, you're sure to hit a framework that practically demands an emotional response.

Here's an example from everyone's favorite[2], *Twilight*, but not from Bella's point of view because, let's face it, she's painfully boring. Here, I've gone ahead and imagined the story from Edward's shiny little perspective:

Who is your character?

Edward Cullen is your typical teen vampire. Good looks, fast car, no pulse.

What is the strange thing going on in their life that throws everything off-kilter and launches the story (the inciting incident)?

Then he meets Bella Swan.

What (or who) do they want most in the world (their objective)?

For the first time, Edward wants a human being more than anything. And he wants her alive.

Who (or what) is in the way of them getting what they want (their obstacle)?

But Edward's bloodlust could drive him to either kill her or turn her into a monster like himself.

What is at stake (vampire pun fully intended) if the character doesn't get what they want?

If Edward doesn't get Bella or, worse, if he hurts her, he'll be alone forever. Literally.

Putting It All Together

Here we go, once again from the top:

Edward Cullen is your typical teen vampire. Good looks, fast car, no pulse. Then he meets Bella Swan. For the first time, Edward wants a human being more than anything. And he wants her alive. But Edward's bloodlust could drive him to either kill her or turn her into a monster like himself. If Edward doesn't get Bella or, worse, if he hurts her, he'll be alone forever. Literally.

Bonus Tip: You will notice that this query meat is one paragraph. I've omitted a lot of detail here. You will want to end up with one to three solid paragraphs of information for the query meat.

Answer these questions about your own manuscript. Read the back and jacket flap copy of published books. Marketing descriptions on any book's online purchase page are also a great guide. By doing this, you will start to internalize the length and tone you're aiming for with a verbal pitch or the meat of your written query.

The most well-crafted queries, in my opinion, are ones that make me *care* about the story and characters. They make me feel something. They make me want to know what happens next.

Agents and editors *want* to hear from writers. They want good projects. They simply can't do their jobs without them. So present the juiciest, most compelling points of your story, mention the important details outlined above, and, finally, keep this whole exercise in perspective. Query letters are just cover letters, even if we've fetishized their role in the publishing process.

You will see many, many examples of query meat in this resource. There's something to learn from each one, and I'm excited to share them with you.

Writing the Synopsis

Many writers hate creating a synopsis—and for good reason. These documents tend to be dry, full of facts, and dull to read. As writers, we always want to add voice to our work. This is nearly impossible in a synopsis. Here's a dirty synopsis secret: If you hate writing it, they will probably hate reading it just as much.

You'll notice that some agents don't even ask for a synopsis. This is good news. The pressure is off! Alas, I would still recommend preparing one, in case someone requests it as part of the submission package or alongside a partial or full manuscript. Just do your best to convey the flow of your story, and you likely won't be evaluated too harshly on this document alone.

Here are some synopsis considerations to keep in mind:

- The synopsis should be either one or two pages, double-spaced. I'd suggest doing an exercise and writing two versions, one short, one long.
- Your synopsis should contain a chronological retelling of your plot.
- If there are big deal character developments, be sure to mention those as well. But that's it.
- Yes, you do need to reveal any plot twists or surprise endings. Agents and publishers will want to see the full scope of your plot. (See the Submission Strategy chapter for more.)
- The tone of the synopsis should be very matter-of-fact. This is *not* a document where you should pitch or tease or withhold information.
- If you find yourself with an overlong synopsis, think of all the things you could delete that, if missing, wouldn't impact the reader's understanding of the core story.
- Clarity is key, above all else. The synopsis should present information, not raise questions or introduce confusion.
- Give your synopsis to a friend or critique partner. Then ask your reader to tell you the gist of your story. If they seem totally confused, it's time to take a second look at your document. Or throw it away and start all over again.
- Now knock it out, worry a bit less, and you'll be on your way!

For a bit more guidance, consider this article:

"How to Write a Novel Synopsis"

---

1. Alas, unless you have the public profile of a Kardashian, you will probably have to write your entire memoir manuscript before trying to sell it. This is why I lump novels (fiction) and memoirs (creative nonfiction) together for submission purposes. Only nonfiction books are generally sold on proposal in today's publishing market.
2. Heavy sarcasm.

QUERY LETTER FORMATTING

THE PREVIOUS CHAPTER detailed the basic query elements as separate ingredients. Now, we will combine them into a formatted query letter. It's true that you can hit these points in your preferred order and there isn't just one way to do it. I'm recommending three options for organizing these components—but mine are not *the only* three options available. Remember that a few elements (like personalization and logline) are optional.

The more information you can include about your project right away (and the more correct and relevant it is), the better. Keep in mind that most queries are going to run between 200-400 words. A query's absolute maximum length is one single-spaced printed page with standard margins.

Bonus Tip: When you see the term "paragraph" below, it may only mean a line or two of material. If you find you have a lot of short paragraphs, you are welcome to combine them.

Here are some options for how I would recommend arranging your query components into a polished letter:

Example Query One:

- PARAGRAPH 1: Personalization
- PARAGRAPH 2: Logline, Comps, Manuscript Logistics
- PARAGRAPHS 3-5: Query Meat
- PARAGRAPH 6: Bio Info
- PARAGRAPH 7: Query Logistics
- Signature

Example Query Two (No Personalization or Logline):

- PARAGRAPH 1: Manuscript Logistics and Comps
- PARAGRAPHS 2-3: Query Meat
- PARAGRAPH 4: Bio Info
- PARAGRAPH 5: Query Logistics
- Signature

Example Query Three (No Logline or Comps):

- PARAGRAPHS 1-3: Query Meat
- PARAGRAPH 4: Bio Info
- PARAGRAPH 5: Personalization and Manuscript Logistics
- PARAGRAPH 6: Query Logistics
- Signature

Query Letter Formatting

Most queries (99% of them) are sent and received via email or submission form these days, so you won't find any outdated advice about SASEs here! In fact, you can completely skip some old-fashioned elements, like the date, recipient address, and sender address at the top of the query. This is a letter writing convention that doesn't play in email.

Simply start with "Dear ..." on the first line. Always use a name, unless you simply cannot find one (a publisher who asks you to target your pitch to the "Submissions Editor" is an example). Depending on your research into agents and publishers, you can decide how formal to be. I'd avoid addressing an agent or editor simply by their first name, but Jane Doe or Ms. Doe are good options. ("Dear Sir" is a bit tone-deaf, since a lot of publishing professionals are women.) Please avoid "To Whom It May Concern."

Queries are traditionally single-spaced. To be email-friendly, they don't use indented first lines. Your best bet is to left-justify everything and use a line break between paragraphs.

End the query with a "Sincerely," and your name, then put your contact info (email, phone, and URL and/or social media credentials, if relevant). If you are including materials like a manuscript or partial manuscript, you can paste that last.

As we will cover in more detail in the next chapter: **copying and pasting is the gold standard, since most agents and publishers do not accept attachments**. Note that copying and pasting from a word processor into email can wreak havoc on formatting, including line spacing and indents. Try it and see what happens. Send an email to yourself first to test how your formatting looks on the receiving end. If the results make you happy, then copy and paste your materials from this email into fresh email messages when you're ready to submit. Copying and pasting from email to email tends to be more foolproof than going from a word processor into email. If your experiment was a misfire, play around with the text within the email compose window.

Agency and publisher submission guidelines differ, but many gatekeepers ask for ten pages or three chapters for a novel or memoir the writing sample. This generally refers to the beginning of the story and includes the prologue, if you have one. **Do not send a random snippet from the middle of the book**, even if "that's where it gets really good." Writing a novel or memoir opening is very hard (this is another book entirely). Don't try to weasel out of exposing your slow or backstory-dense beginning by sending a snapshot of your climax instead.

Picture book manuscripts are generally sent in their entirety, as are book proposals.

The next chapter will briefly discuss two specific topics—manuscript formatting and illustrations—which might pertain to your submission package. After we've assembled everything you need, we will touch on agent research and submission strategy. Then—it's query time!

MANUSCRIPT FORMATTING AND ILLUSTRATIONS

WHILE NOT ALL query letter writers will find this section useful, and while this book isn't technically about manuscript formatting or illustration or book proposals or other query-adjacent topics, I'd be remiss if I entirely neglected these elements that frequently accompany the query.

All writing sample materials (and synopses) are generally double-spaced, whereas the query letter is single-spaced. The manuscript itself should have new lines indented to .5″ (with the exception of the first line of a new chapter, which can be justified left, as a stylistic choice). The project document should have a separate title page with your title, word count, name, and contact information. The file should have standard 1″ margins and use 12-point font (Times New Roman or similar).

New chapters generally appear after a page break and five or six blank lines down the page. Chapter headings, whether numbers or names, are popular and can help keep your project organized. I'd specifically recommend them if you have multiple POVs (points of view) or are weaving together different narrative chronologies.

Here's a quick example of what manuscript formatting might look like for a standard novel:

[Page 1]

My Great Book!
YA Fantasy, 90,000 Words

BY MARY KOLE

(Contact Information)

[Page Break]

[PAGE 2]

CHAPTER 1

This is the beginning of my chapter. Please pretend that this is double-spaced. Otherwise, this is exactly how I'd format my manuscript.

"I'd also make sure to include dialogue," said Mary, "because action is such a crucial part of a novel opening. But that's a story for another book."

"What if we're writing nonfiction?" Writer McWriterface asked.

"Narrative style works in some nonfiction, too!" said The Exception to Every Rule.

"We are not doing this, guys." Mary threatened to throw the laptop across the room. "This book is about query letters."

"Okay, okay, okay," they said in unison. "We'll behave."

(Amazing prose continues. Trust me, it's the best thing ever written.)

When you are fulfilling a full or partial manuscript request and the agent or publisher explicitly asks for an attachment, you should send the document in .doc or .docx format (.pages and other program-specific formats are not crowd-pleasers) or PDF (preferred if you have some unique formatting or layout that you need to preserve).

Bonus Tip: You don't have to send *exactly* ten pages (or three chapters, or whatever the submission guidelines request) alongside your query, as formatting tends to vary. Most of your email submissions will end up looking single-spaced, anyways. You should send ten double-spaced pages *worth* of material, or close to it. You can also finish a chapter, even if that means you send slightly more than what the guidelines specify. Nobody is going to double-check. (The unfortunate reality is that most agents and publishers will know whether or not they're going to like the material after a paragraph or two. Some won't reach the end of the sample, so you're getting worked up for nothing.)

If you simply can't figure out how to make your query or writing sample look nice in email, don't sweat it *too much*. Pasting into a query submission form can make even the most beautifully formatted document look downright tragic. You will not be the biggest disaster in a gatekeeper's inbox on any given day, trust me. Besides, while a nice-looking submission doesn't hurt, your pitch is more about substance than style. Just do the best you can.

Illustrations and Picture Book Dummies

This section will mostly refer to picture book projects, but I acknowledge that other kinds of books have visual or design elements that their creators will want considered alongside the text.

If you are planning to illustrate your book project, or have hired someone to provide visual assets[1], you should have the following components ready before submission:

- the query letter;
- a copy of the picture book text as a standalone manuscript file;
- and a "sketch dummy" of the full picture book with two or three "mock finishes" *or* a fully designed prototype of the concept, if it's not a picture book.

The "sketch dummy" refers to a PDF of the entire picture book, paginated and laid out as it would appear in print form. However, the illustrations are not finished, which lets the creator submit without taking the time to finish each spread. This is strategic, as revisions might be suggested down the road, and the illustrations will have to be redone. Loose black and white pencil or other sketches are fine here.

PDF is the most popular format for complete books, while individual images can be sent as .jpg, .jpeg, or .png files.

The term "mock finishes" refers to two or three pages of the dummy which get the full color "finished" treatment. The dummy should also include the text overlaid or otherwise paginated and positioned on the pages.

For any project with a visual component, your submission package would not be considered complete without your intended illustrations.

But this is where many artists and designers run into a big problem. How do you transmit your dummy and/or images without sending an unsolicited attachment?

The solution is to host your work online. But take heart, I don't mean that you should post it widely for (potentially) all to see, especially if you feel protective over your idea. Instead, I recommend hosting the relevant files on your website and then either sending around a download link, or putting them on a page that's password protected and sending login credentials in the query. That way, you limit public exposure.

You can also upload files to Google Drive, Dropbox, iCloud, WeTransfer, or a similar cloud-based document storage service and send a direct download link in the query. Note that some of these services have file size limits (picture book dummies tend to be big files) or download expiration dates. If your file link expires after a week, an agent will very likely not be looking at it within that timeframe, so be extra sure that you are aware of any restrictions to the upload/download process. I'd personally reconsider sending any link that expires, period. Make it easy for the agent or publisher to consider you, and erase all potential barriers. If the link is broken, they can't access the file, the permission are invalid, etc., the gatekeeper might decide that your project isn't worth the hassle.

If you're an aspiring illustrator, think beyond the project-specific dummy. You should also put up an online portfolio with at least five sample images that reflect all of your different styles and talents.

Consider rounding out your portfolio with some characters, scenes, as well as full bleed spreads and spot illustrations. While you may want to keep a dummy private, a general portfolio should be widely available for viewing, especially if you are going to be directing agents and art directors to your website.

For some free picture book dummy template downloads, head over to:

goodstorycompany.com/pb-vip

Otherwise, let's dig into submission strategy!

---

1. Do you "have to" illustrate a picture book or hire an illustrator before submission? No. Publishers like to select illustrators—and will *pay for the art*. Commissioning illustrations can be very expensive, especially if you want something that looks good. This question is beyond the scope of this particular book but I did want to clarify.

SUBMISSION STRATEGY

MANY WRITERS FIXATE on the query letter itself as they prepare to submit their work to literary agents and publishers, but it's also important to develop a strong and intentional submission strategy.

Below, I'll discuss a few submission-specific concepts and considerations for you to keep in mind.

Simultaneous Submission

Everyone should be doing simultaneous submissions instead of exclusives (with one small caveat). This simply means that you're sending your query or proposal to more than one agent or publisher at a time. Why? Publishing takes forever. Agents are known to sit on projects for months and then still ghost you. If you submit to person after person exclusively, you may wait years to collect all of the responses you're going to get. This is not efficient, and it doesn't behoove you.

Sure, agents like to consider things without competition. It levels the playing field. But I would never, ever offer something exclusively if it hasn't been requested that way first. Simultaneous submissions are par for the course in today's publishing business. Now, there are agents and publishers out there that will *only* consider submissions sent to them exclusively. It's up to you if you want to submit to those people or houses. I might not, if it was my project. I'd hate to tie it up in someone's inbox for four to six weeks unnecessarily.

The *one* exception is if you've spent time with one agent or editor in particular, doing revision based on their notes, even if they haven't yet offered a representation agreement or book contract. This means an agent or publisher liked your idea but requested some changes before committing—otherwise known as a "revise and resubmit." If you use their suggestions to do a revision, it's only fair to give them an exclusive opportunity to consider the resulting project. If they still pass, all bets are off, and you can approach a wider audience simultaneously.

When I was agenting, people would send me exclusive submissions that I hadn't requested. Querying isn't like the early decision or early action college admissions process. An unsolicited exclusive submission doesn't help your case. Take a more strategic approach and submit simultaneously to more than one party at a time. As long as you mention this in your query, you are welcome to do it.

Bonus Tip: Many writers wonder if they can submit to literary agents and publishers that accept unagented submissions at the same time. I say yes. It's very unlikely that an agent will call to offer representation on the same day that a publisher will extend a contract. The wheels of publishing move very slowly. So you can build both agents and publishers (that accept unagented work) into your simultaneous submission strategy. That being said, if you receive an offer of representation from an agent or word that a publisher is planning to extend a book deal, you will want to let everyone else know. If you get a publishing contract, resist the urge to accept the exact terms (or the offer itself) if you are still waiting to hear from agents. Those agents may want to step in and negotiate on your behalf. If you've already accepted the contract terms in your excitement, there's nothing for the agent to do, and they might be less enthused to work with you.

(The boilerplate contract many publishers offer to unagented writers is often very favorable to the publisher, and not favorable at all to the writer, since the writer doesn't have any negotiating leverage. This is why many creators want to try and get an agent first.)

Revealing Your Twist or Ending in the Query Letter

Agents and publishers want to see how your plotting brain works, especially if you're writing a high-concept novel in a category like mystery or thriller. And yet most writers don't want to reveal their book's ending in a query letter or synopsis. This is understandable.

The assumption is this: If I can hook them with the query, they'll simply *have* to request the entire manuscript. Right? Unfortunately, wrong.

Even the most tantalizing, anxiety-provoking query won't make a busy literary agent want to read 300 pages unless they are otherwise compelled to do so. Humans like intrigue, but they don't like intrigue enough to sink five hours of reading into every query letter that promises a big tease. It's just not feasible.

So reveal your big twist. Pull back the curtain on your shocking ending. Use the query to show agents and publishers that you can *plot your patootie off*. Excite them with the idea of *what* you do in the story, then make them want to see *how* you do it. That's a tease *with substance*, and much more evocative than cheap mystery.

Of course, there are some queries in this resource that don't reveal the ending. This is not a hard and fast rule, and it doesn't apply to everyone.

See how other writers have done it in the example queries, and pick the approach that's right for your project.

Writing and Submitting a Series

This is a writing issue, not a query issue, but it warrants discussion. As a former agent, I am a bit negative about series from a debut talent. Writers love them. Obviously, it's a much stronger pitch to offer three books rather than one, right? Plus, then you have three books under contract, you're paid three times as much, and you really become a valuable asset to your publisher. (And, creatively, you can spend two or more books developing your unique story and characters, not just one!) Well, in theory, yes ...

The real power position, however, is to write a manuscript that has series potential and can be expanded but primarily stands alone. Then your publisher champions it, it does well, readers react with overwhelming praise, and the house asks you for a sequel. The support is already there, and chances are that the entire series will perform better because the publisher is begging for more, instead of you crawling to them with your hands clasped.

The last thing you want is to sell a trilogy, have the first book underperform, and then be faced with a publisher who has no enthusiasm for books two and three. They're just doing it to fulfill a contract, and internally, they've likely already moved on to other, more promising properties. This, unfortunately, happens all the time. And the debut writer's play for job security ends up backfiring in a big way.

If you simply *require* three books to tell your story, there's no way around it, I suppose. But if there's any wiggle room here (and there probably should be, since you're making up the whole idea and can call all the shots), I'd highly encourage you to take the "one strong story that mostly resolves in a way that's satisfying for readers" approach and pitch it as a project with "series potential" in the query.

Choosing Your Book's Category

People generally start out writing a story because it grips them. They don't think a lot about their reading audience or publishing category. Some writers have a strong sense of category in mind even before they put fingers to keys. There's no wrong entry into a book project, and you shouldn't let market inform your decisions, unless you want it to. But at some point, I would encourage you to think about your category and readership, if you haven't already.

You will notice that your category is a key part of your pitch. You want to make sure and mention whether you're writing YA or literary fiction, memoir or picture book. This will absolutely dictate which agents and publishers you choose to approach, so it's important knowledge for you to have. You should also endeavor to read in your chosen category, so that you know whether you're writing something potentially marketable.

For example, anyone is free to write a five-hundred-page picture book. (To be clear, the gold standard picture book length is thirty-two pages.) Anyone can do whatever they want. But if you start to learn about the picture book category—and that nobody is actually publishing such long projects—you will realize that your odds of *succeeding* with a five-hundred-page picture book are very slim. (I really want to say "nonexistent" here, but I've been wrong before!)

Some writers think it's appealing to pitch their oddball, category-destroying project with the words, "Nobody's doing anything like this!" I understand why. It sounds compelling. But learning about various publishing categories might actually reveal that you're taking a big risk. Publishers aren't generally publishing oddball projects either, for one or two reasons. First, they've either tried and failed already, or, second, they've concluded that there's no market for that type of book. So if "Nobody's doing anything like this!" is the cornerstone of your pitch, make sure it's really an attribute, rather than a liability.

Some writers also think that pitching a book "for ages zero to one hundred, anyone and everyone" makes their project sound more marketable. This is an easy mistake to make. Why not sell a book to everyone on the planet, after all? Eight billion copies sold would make for a handsome royalty check! Well, most marketers and publishers know that the wider the audience, the more difficult the sale. If you are able to locate a more specific target demographic, this is actually much more desirable than trying to sell your story to anyone and everyone. Choosing a definitive category also makes you sound a bit less naïve.

Suggesting "Crossover Appeal"

The idea of a "crossover" book is often mentioned when the conversation turns to publishing category, but it leaves some writers confused. It means a children's book that appeals to the wider general fiction "adult" market (or vice versa). Here, I don't mean "adult" as in "erotica," I just mean "non-children's."

The Book Thief by Markus Zusak is an example of a crossover book that was published for both middle grade and adult readers. Many titles that were originally published as MG and YA, like *The Hunger Games* by Suzanne Collins, cross over to an older readership.

Another meaning of this term is a literary fiction book that could play well in the trade market space. Books that may have originally been intended for a smaller audience, like *The Help* by Kathryn Sockett, will often cross over as publisher support for them builds, or if there's a movie in the works.

The thing to note about "crossover" is that it's not something you, the writer, can manufacture. Especially not at the query phase. A crossover hit will either be created by your publisher (when they see excitement for the project from a book buyer account, in-house marketing, or Hollywood), or it will happen organically after publication, due to reader response.

To pitch something as "crossover," again, conveys that your market knowledge and expectations are perhaps a bit unrealistic.

NOW THAT YOU ARE PRETTY MUCH A QUERY BASICS GENIUS, LET'S LEARN about those gatekeepers, shall we?

AGENT AND PUBLISHER RESEARCH RESOURCES

SO WHERE DOES a writer with a great book find their literary agent or publishing house match? I highly recommend the following resources for researching your submission targets. Some of the most serious mistakes that writers make happen in the research phase, so spend some time here. Don't put anyone and everyone on your list. Be selective. You're going to potentially be working with an agent or publisher for years, so don't let your excitement to submit or your desire to be accepted cloud your judgment.

Online Resources

Everything in the publishing landscape has moved online, so these will likely be the most important tools in your arsenal.

MANUSCRIPT WISH LIST:

manuscriptwishlist.com

A great and frequently updated resource that collects wish lists from agents and publishers. Add this to your research and see if you can catch the right gatekeeper at the right time with your project. Also check out the #MSWL hashtag.

THE ASSOCIATION OF AMERICAN LITERARY AGENTS:

aalitagents.org

The Association of American Literary Agents (AALA, formerly the AAR) lists of member agencies that have joined and agree to abide by ethics codes and standards.

ABSOLUTE WRITE WATER COOLER:

absolutewrite.com/forums/index.php

Absolute Write is a message board serving all types of writers. You'll find threads for the agent search, response times, industry rumors, and craft topics, of course. A great place to vent and get the inside scoop from other people on the submission trail.

AGENT QUERY:

agentquery.com

A searchable database of agents that allows you to search by genre and category. Want someone who represents both fantasy and young adult? Check the boxes and see who fits your criteria. Results give you contact information, submission guidelines, and a sample listing of that agent's recent sales.

QUERY TRACKER:

querytracker.net

This is a similar website to Agent Query (above), but it also lets you organize and track your query and submission status. If you're very motivated, you can see what other writers are logging for response dates to try and puzzle out what an agent is doing in their inbox.

Publishers Marketplace:

publishersmarketplace.com

This paid resource ($25/month as of this writing) is pure gold. It's a comprehensive database that tracks book deals across many categories and genres. I recommend that all writers who are serious about their agent and publisher research join for at least one month while putting together their submission lists (you can cancel at any time). (Full disclosure: I do not receive any financial consideration for recommending this particular resource, it's simply the best and most comprehensive database out there.)

You can see who's selling what, how much, how often, to which publishers, etc. Almost all agents sound great on paper (and on their websites), but I think track record is more telling. Same for publishers. Who is doing deals in your category?

Each entry also describes a book's logline, which can help you figure out the types of stories that are being bought and sold right now. Publishing people sit around looking at "PM" (as it's know in the industry) all day—and the announcements listed here are helping publishing gatekeepers make their decisions.

Book Resources

The books listed in this section are updated regularly, so make sure you pick up the most recent edition. One is the *Writer's Digest Guide to Literary Agents*. Another is the *Writer's Market* guide. There's also *Jeff Herman's Guide to Book Publishers, Editors, and Literary Agents*.

It's important to note that the above resources also contain information about publishers. If you are thinking of querying publishers directly instead of (or in addition to) literary agents, you can use these directories to find independent, small, niche, and regional publishers that take unagented submissions.

Literary Agency Websites

It behooves a literary agency to have a detailed website. The agency wants to attract good submissions, after all. Great projects are their bread and butter. No research round is complete without a visit to the corresponding agency website for each gatekeeper that you plan on targeting (to read about individual agents *and* get submission guidelines).

Agent Social Media

Agents have to attract new clients to make a living. It's therefore advantageous for them to be active on social media. Agents often write articles, do interviews, or record podcast appearances as well. Google the agent's name and see what you can learn about them that isn't part of their official agency bio. See what they're saying about themselves online, and see what others have to say about them. (There are, unfortunately, a lot of jilted writers out there, so you might not take everything you read as gospel, especially if it's overly complimentary or derogatory.) You may find nuggets of information that you can use to make a specific connection in your query personalization section (though I'd be wary of making it *too* personal, again).

Publisher Websites

If a publisher is accepting submissions from the general public, they'll have a section devoted to that endeavor on their website. After all, they want to attract targeted submissions that fit their needs. Pay careful attention to whether that publisher has several imprints (or divisions), and how they prefer to receive materials.

Different imprints will have their own titles, approaches, and editorial teams. Some smaller publishers have several imprints, but the same acquiring editor will see every submission. Some larger publishers don't have any overlap.

Bonus Tip: When you start to research publishers and decide to submit directly to them instead of getting a literary agent first, you may be tempted to type "publisher" or "publisher accepting submissions" into Google and see where that gets you. Be very aware that most of the publishers you'll find by doing this are self-publishing, for-profit, vanity, or hybrid publishers. The exact definition of these terms is beyond the scope of this book, but they all have one thing in common: they will charge you money to publish your work. They will likely not pay any kind of advance, either, and they'll take a higher royalty percentage of each sale, if they offer a royalty at all. Many of them have slick, wonderful websites that boast about their clients' successful books, happy authors, glowing testimonials, etc. They will all look very legitimate, and many of them *are* actual publishers, in the sense that they produce book-shaped objects. (Of course, there is a ton of variability here. There are some very professional and reputable hybrid publishers, but what differentiates them from traditional publishers is that they charge for their services.) If this is the kind of arrangement you're seeking, great! But if you are looking for traditional publishers that do not charge content creators up-front fees, you will likely come up short with this kind of search.

Now, let's discuss the process of putting everything together and actually going on submission.

SUBMISSION PROCESS

HERE'S my recommended submission roadmap so that you can make the most of putting your manuscript in front of gatekeepers.

Getting Everything Ready

Ideally, you are going to use the tools in the Agent and Publisher Research Resources chapter to come up with a list of literary agents and publishers (or both at the same time, see the Submission Strategy chapter) that you genuinely believe might be interested in your project.

You'll want to research and finalize a list of about twenty-five or thirty agents and/or publishers. Then you will separate these names into an "A List" (the people you really want to work with) and a "B List" (others you've researched and are excited about).

You should then visit everyone's website one last time to collect each agent or publisher's submission guidelines. Agencies and publishers will be very specific about these details, because they want to see uniform submissions that (they hope) will meet their standards.

You can keep track of submission guidelines as you build your submission list with a handy submission tracker spreadsheet I created, which you can find here:

"Submission Tracker Spreadsheet"

To use this for your own purposes, go to the "File" menu, and then select "Make a copy ..." This will repurpose this document on your own Google Drive and allow you to edit it.

Bonus Tip: Sometimes you will fall in love with an agent, only to discover at the last minute that they have closed to queries, gone on leave, or left the business. Alas, this happens. There isn't much you can do about it unless you want to delay your entire submission round, or your submission to this one gatekeeper. Yes, this unexpected news can be a bitter pill to swallow, but don't let it stop you.

The more thorough your research process, the more likely you're going to turn up information that will be useful to you when you're personalizing your query letter. For example, you should note the titles of books that the agent or publisher has worked on, and link them to your work. You can also take note of things an agent has said in an interview, or a recent #MSWL request that aligns with your manuscript.

Once you know what to send and where to send it, you will put together a custom submission package for each target, starting with a personalized version of your query, if you're using that element.

Now there's nothing left to do open up the expertly prepared submission packages you've personalized to your "A List" of dream agents and publishers ... and click "Send."

Must Do Tip: Submit to only one agent per agency and one imprint per publisher (for publishers that have more than one division) at a time. If that agent or imprint passes, you can reconsider your options. But you will wipe out big time if you send to every agent at an agency at once. This is why research is crucial.

OMG I SENT IT! OMG, Now What?

One of the weirdest feelings in the world is the primal rush of terror and excitement that accompanies a life-changing (as we've convinced ourselves it will be) submission …

And then the almost soul-sucking, astronaut-floating-alone-in-space silence that follows.

It's true, some agents will get back to you in, like, five minutes with a rejection or a request. Huh? *Did they even read it?*

Most likely. But sometimes, if you're working in rhyming picture books about vampires and the particular representative hates both verse and vamps, they will fire off a "no" fast enough to make your head spin. That's okay.

This is your time to *wait,* and this is the hardest part. But don't be tempted to react with excitementerror[1] every time your email dings. And certainly don't take every single pass to heart. Or every single piece of feedback as gospel truth. I counsel writers all the time against getting one comment on their novel and ripping the whole thing apart that same day to address it.

Your job is to wait.

Most agencies and publishers will specify a response timeframe (six to eight weeks is a good ballpark). Sometimes they will get back to you. Sometimes "no news means no."

Sometimes you will get a revise and resubmit letter (see more about these in the Submission Strategy chapter). Sometimes you might get an offer of representation! Sometimes you might get several! All of these positive outcomes will be unique to you and your project, and these more advanced topics of revision and working with a literary agent are beyond the scope of this book.

So let's move on to the somewhat more likely (don't shoot the messenger) scenario—the submission isn't successful. You don't receive an offer of representation or a book contract. And, believe it or not, that's okay.

There *are* a few things you can do to emerge triumphant—once you peel yourself off the floor, shake the cat out of your lap, and wipe the Ben & Jerry's off of your ratty old high school marching band comfort shirt, of course.

The next step is to put all of your feedback together and see if a pattern emerges.

Next Steps After an Unsuccessful Submission

Every submission round is unique. So are the next steps available to you if your query wasn't successful. It all depends on whether you got specific rejections *with feedback*, or not. The more specific feedback you receive, the more closely your work was considered. Some writers will get a few sentences along the lines of "I didn't connect with the voice" and believe this was personal.

I'm afraid it's usually not, but agents and publishers know that voice is such a nebulous and subjective thing that nobody can really argue with this assessment. A truly personal rejection will mention elements of the story itself, call characters by name, or make revision suggestions that feel targeted to the substance of the project.

Read more about the different types of rejection (yes, there are different types!) in this article:

"Types of Rejection Letters and Query Rejection"

If there is actionable feedback in your "declines" (a nice industry term for rejections), you might have something concrete to work with.

Decide if the notes resonate, and if they do, you can decide whether you want to revise by yourself or get a critique group or freelance editor to help you.

If you are getting only form rejections, this is a sign that your project simply isn't ready, or that the premise isn't hitting.

Once you've completed one unsuccessful submission round and a pretty substantial revision of your project, you can try submitting it to the agents on your "B List," as well as any agents who you still want to target from your "A List."

This will be your next submission. I always advocate for smaller submission rounds of ten or fifteen well-targeted names because you never know what kind of feedback you'll get. This allows you to be more responsive, without burning through every available target.

If you find that you receive a consistent critique of your project, but you've already sent it to every single agent who represents your category, you're a bit SOL.

I realize submission is exciting and most writers can't wait to find out what'll happen with their projects. But slow and steady—backed by strong research—often wins the race.

The Resubmission Question

You may notice, above, that I'm seemingly okay with resubmitting to agents who have previously seen—and passed on— the work. Haven't you already blown it with your "A List"?

Not necessarily. In fact, it's perfectly possible to submit to agents who have already rejected you, but *only* if you can honestly say that you've done a pretty big revision of the project.

Your target initially passed for a reason, whether they expressed that reason to you or not. If you send them the same manuscript with a light revision (moving commas around, mostly), they will probably pass again. But if you've gotten great feedback from your submission round *and* you've fundamentally revised, you can absolutely try to resubmit.

Be sure to mention in your second query letter that the agent or publisher has seen this project before, but that you've made significant changes. The worst they can do is say "no" once more. This is a low-risk gamble with a lot of potential upside, especially if the agent or publisher offered you some personal feedback the first time around. That means there was some interest there initially that you could potentially capitalize on.

Bonus Tip: Is a "no" from one agent or editor a "no from all" at that agency or publisher, respectively? You will often see this mentioned on an agency or publisher website. It means that a "no" from one person puts the whole company off-limits. For agencies, this may not be true. Most agents maintain their own slush piles, especially if they have a unique, personal email address for slush[2]. (Some agencies keep generic submission inboxes, though, so this advice doesn't apply.) If an agent has rejected you and you can be somewhat sure that they're the only person at the agency who has seen your work, you can add a different agent from the same company to your "B List" for the next submission round. It's not an illegal move. For publishers, it's harder to tell because you have no way of knowing who actually reviewed your submission. A resubmission may land in front of the same editor (or intern) who declined it the first time, so sending a project back to a publisher who already passed is more of a gamble.

To Recap the Submission Process

Remember, your submission strategy is crucial to getting out into the world with your manuscript, so let's summarize it here, once more from the top, with a rehash of the pre-submission steps for good measure:

1. Write the very best manuscript you can, with an eye toward the market for your potential idea. **The biggest mistakes are made at this point**, especially if you aren't yet intentional about what you're writing or who you're writing it for.
2. Bring all of your writing craft knowledge to bear on a killer revision of said manuscript. Writers are notoriously bad at seeing issues with their own work, so it's best to involve a second set of eyes, whether a critique partner, writing group, beta reader, or freelance editor.
3. Revise, like, ten more times.
4. Get very, very sick of your project.
5. Put it aside for a month. (No, seriously!)
6. Revise *one last time*[3]!
7. Agonize over the query letter and synopsis as you put your submission package together.
8. Read this guide again and get clarity on your query! Whew!
9. Stare at the wall and reconsider all of the life choices that led you to this point.
10. Do very solid agent and publisher research and make your "A List" and "B List." **A lot of mistakes are made at this point as well**, especially as anticipation and impatience assert themselves.
11. Ride a bizarre emotional rollercoaster, convinced you're either a genius or a hack. Or sometimes both, all within the same moment.
12. Put together your submissions, paying attention to individual submission guidelines and formatting (to the best of your ability).
13. Press "Send" on your emails and forms!
14. Hear back, usually over the course of weeks or months. You should have all the responses you're going to get after four months.
15. See step 9.
16. Scrape together the feedback you've gotten. (Remember: a complete lack of personalized feedback is also feedback, in and of itself.) See if you can spot any patterns.

17. Make a revision plan or decide to "take the wisdom and leave the rest" from this particular project and put it away, either temporarily or permanently.
18. Either enact your revision plan or work on something new.
19. See step 9.
20. If you're sticking with the project, put together your next submission round, calling on your "B List" and any targets from your "A List" who seemed promising.
21. Don't forget to come up for air, read for pleasure, talk to humans, and do some self-care. (If you figure out this whole work-life balance thing, let me know.)

And there it is, in all of its glory. The submission process. Things do get pretty outcome-dependent after about step sixteen, but this is as accurate a generalization as I can offer.

---

1. Patent pending.
2. Mine used to be "marysqueries"!
3. Just kidding. If you land an agent, you'll likely revise again. A book deal? More revision. You'd do well to learn to love it ASAP because revision isn't going anywhere.

HOW TO USE THIS BOOK

ONCE YOU GET into the example query letters that follow, you will notice that they are annotated. I employ a few different marks throughout. In an editorial setting, I would be using Word's Track Changes function to correct the text and make margin notes. In book form, I've experimented with the formatting to replicate this editorial mark-up. Here's a key:

Underlines

If you see underlines, they mean one of two things. First, I might be pointing out "word echo," or word/phrase repetition in close proximity. The second is redundancy, or the writer is expressing the same thought in two or more ways (a great example would be this explanation). Queries have low word counts, so I always recommend getting rid of word echo and repetition for a tighter letter.

Footnotes

My more specific comments can be found in footnotes, which appear immediately following the example query text. Each footnote appears directly after the part I'm talking about. I will either comment on a single word or phrase, or a full sentence or passage. The latter will be isolated with [brackets], with the footnote coming directly after the closing bracket. The associated comment will refer to that portion of the query.

Brackets

Per the above, [brackets] tie together a passage or idea for the purposes of a comment.

Bold and Strikethrough Formatting

My additions or direct changes to the text will appear in **bold**. The things I suggest omitting from the original letter will appear with ~~strikethrough formatting~~.

Parentheses

If part of a query has been redacted by the writer, that part will either appear as a generic word, for example, "My book, TITLE …," or in parentheses, for example, "I'm writing to you because (personalization)."

Be aware that the writer probably had more specific content here but has chosen to omit this passage from the example query. I have chosen to redact all names and contact information, except for those identifying details that the writer has granted permission to share.

Summary Feedback Chapters

A short overview note that summarizes my main thoughts and findings appears in a separate chapter immediately following each sample query.

If you are working on novel-length fiction, I do want to point out that you will find relevant novel queries in several places. Thought we've already talked about the difference between the terms "children's books" and "adult books," I want to reiterate that these distinctions refer to the age of the target audience, rather than to "adult content."

Fiction writers can look at the Middle Grade section, the Young Adult section, as well as the Fiction section (this distinction is made to separate fiction for adult readers from fiction for young readers).

Don't let the fact that these novels are written for kid readers turn you off—some of the middle grade and young adult examples reprinted here are among the strongest query letters in this guide!

Now, please enjoy the annotated query letters and respective feedback chapters that follow. They are collected here by category and genre for ease of reference!

Picture Book Queries

PICTURE BOOK QUERY #1 (190 WORDS)

DEAR MS. ORR (Rachel Orr at Prospect Agency),

[Things have changed since Violet's brother came along, but it isn't the baby Violet is worried about][1]. [It's MOMBIE! She grunts and groans, smells awful, and never sleeps ... like a zombie!][2] When MOMBIE starts gobbling the baby's toes and sniffing behind his ears, Violet springs into action to get her mom back!

MOMBIE, a 370-word picture book, [offers a fresh perspective on how a new baby in the house challenges existing relationships][3]. It is MONKEY BROTHER by Adam Auerbach meets **Kelly** DiPucchio's[4] ZOMBIE **IN** LOVE 2+1.

[I am submitting my work to you because of your interest in punchy, humorous text with a strong marketing hook. I value the editorial expertise you bring to your role, and enjoy the work of your clients Cori Doerrfeld and Sudipta Bardhan-Quallen][5].

I have been a member of SCBWI since 2013 and [have a Master's in Early Childhood Education][6]. I was a recipient of a 2017 Writing With The Stars mentorship and have participated in Julie Hedlund's 12X12 Picture Book Challenge for four years.

Please note that this is a simultaneous submission. Thank you for your consideration of my manuscript MOMBIE, included below.

Sincerely,

(Signature)

---

1. The writer jumps right into the story with two immediate zaps of tension. Things have changed (kids hate change!), and yet the baby is *not* the problem. This piques my curiosity because it's a clever reversal.
2. Great introduction to the premise.
3. Some thematic analysis is expected for picture book queries, because picture books usually have a universal theme that writers are playing with. The birth of a sibling is a popular picture book sales hook.
4. I'd mention the full name here.
5. Strong personalization!
6. This is exactly the kind of relevant bio paragraph detail that connects the writer to what they're writing.

PICTURE BOOK QUERY #1 FEEDBACK

A HOME RUN picture book query that everyone should try to emulate. Not only is the premise funny and fresh, but there is strong attention paid to market hook. New siblings happen to a lot of picture book readers, so there's a big appetite for books that address the topic. However, because it is *such* a common idea, there's competition. Finding a unique spin on a popular idea is just the ticket for a crowded marketplace.

This query's focus on sales hook and theme is especially important in picture book pitches. The length is a winner, too. Note that the query is just under 200 words. There's no need to go longer, since the manuscript will be included with the pitch, so the agent or publisher can scroll right down and read on, if interested.

PICTURE BOOK QUERY #2 (130 WORDS)

Dear Agent,

[George Georgian is used to getting what he wants][1]. So when his friends **don't** come immediately at his command, he throws the biggest, most animal-like fit. But every time ~~his~~ Manny[2] tells him to wait, [George Georgian steps his tantrum up a notch. Will he ever figure out that maybe, just maybe, his friends are afraid of his noise][3]?

GEORGE GEORGIAN AND A ROYAL BEDTIME[4] is a light-hearted picture book for children (3-5)[5] and is complete at 750[6] words. It will appeal to fans of *No Fits, Nilson!* and *Mouse Was Mad*. I am a diverse writer.

The full manuscript is pasted below my name and email, per your submission guidelines. Please note that this is a simultaneous submission. Thank you very much for your time and consideration.

Sincerely,

(Signature)

1. The biggest concern I have here is whether this character will be relatable and fun to read. Or is he going to be unsympathetic? Sure, tantrums are a daily reality for the target picture book audience. But readers have to see some glimmer of a sympathetic protagonist before they'll latch on to his story. Maybe soften him like this, "Even though he's a great buddy, George ..."
2. "Dad," "Mom," "Manny," "Grandma," etc. are only capitalized if used in place of a name. Compare "Hey, Mom! How's it going?" to "I need to ask my mom if I can come over." This writer uses "his Manny" but if "Manny" stands for "man nanny," then it's a nickname. The writer can either omit the "his," as I've done here, or say "his manny" (lowercase).
3. I'd avoid the rhetorical question approach. This is the writer's chance to pitch *their* story. Even though this phrasing raises stakes, I'd much rather know *how* this writer lands this particular tale, instead of being asked to hypothetically imagine what might happen. In picture books, especially, the writer will want to give the reader a sense of the resolution, because this communicates the book's theme or message.
4. Wait, this is jarring. The entire above paragraph is about friends and tantrums. This is the first mention of bedtime. Bedtime books are their own picture book category. This makes me wonder if I'm missing something.
5. Redundant here. Picture books are primarily for kids ages three to five. So saying "picture book for children (3-5)" presents the same information three times. Just say "picture book," which will convey the target audience to any publishing professional. The writer should also spell out ages as words, not numerals, should they choose to use them.
6. The project's word count is quite long for the market and this is a potential concern.

PICTURE BOOK QUERY #2 FEEDBACK

THERE'S a disconnect between the pitch and the title that really throws me for a loop. If there's a bedtime angle, tackle that right up front. Bedtime books are considered their own special slice of the picture book market, and can be a sales hook.

Otherwise, the writer should really consider how they intend to sell readers on George as a character, even though he throws tantrums. Right now, there's nothing redeeming to balance how his behavior is described.

Finally, be very clear about the resolution. While writers don't want to go too heavy-handed with the message in the manuscript itself, picture books do tend to touch upon universal topics of parenting and growing up, and agents and publishers will want to know the themes you're working with. Consider these articles:

"Books That Teach Life Lessons"

"How to Write Child Characters With Their Own Wisdom"

PICTURE BOOK QUERY #3 (278 WORDS)

Dear Agent,

(A personalized opening statement here.) [I saw that you're open to picture book submissions, and that you're a fan of slightly humorous and quirky][1]. I'm pleased to submit my **600-word**[2] picture book, LUCKY TRUCK.

[Most people think gnomes belong in the garden. But did you know some say mining gnomes exist, and that they bring good luck?][3] In LUCKY TRUCK, Marshall and his new toy truck are mining for gold because Marshall loves being a miner, just like his dad. Suddenly, Lucky Truck is gone! Strange noises grow louder. [RAP, RAP. TAP, TAP. TINK, TINK, TINK,][4] leads Marshall to a mining gnome, named Diggety Dan, who has added a little magic to Lucky Truck. But[5] Diggety Dan decides to take the truck![6] Marshall tries every mining trick and worries he'll never see Lucky Truck again. Then he gets an ingenious idea [to use his mining toys to create the ultimate trap][7]. Not only does Marshall get his special truck back, but he turns it[8] into a happy little twist on teamwork. [Other comps might be Ashley Anstee's NO, NO GNOME! and Adam Wallace's HOW TO CATCH A LEPRECHAUN][9].

[I have three picture book titles, a non-fiction chapter book, and an award-winning middle grade history mystery, all listed below][10]. I'm a long-time SCBWI member, run a writer's critique group, and have organized the Barnes & Noble "Boulder Children's Writers Festival" and "Dust to Dust Jackets," a historical MG panel discussion. I've also conducted writing workshops for children and adults and spoken at conferences and numerous schools, so I'll put my best marketing efforts behind LUCKY TRUCK.

Please find the complete manuscript pasted below. This is a simultaneous submission. Thank you for considering representation.

(Signature)

(List of Manuscripts/Publications, per the above)

---

1. Good personalization! This is specific and shows the writer has done their research.
2. If the writer wants to use this phrasing, they will want to hyphenate it.
3. Given that the title "LUCKY TRUCK" is all I know about the project, the shift in gears to gnomes is a bit jarring. It takes a while (halfway through this paragraph) to see how the truck and the gnome collide. Is there a smoother transition possible?
4. Onomatopoeia is usually formatted in italics, though caps can work for an email or submission form query, especially if the writer is worried that their formatting won't translate. Including some noises in the query tells me that there will be good read-aloud potential, which is a sales hook with picture book.
5. I'd maybe consider breaking the query meat into two paragraphs here.
6. Didn't he already take the truck? ("Suddenly, Lucky Truck is gone!")
7. Spelling out the exact solution itself may be too detailed for the purposes of the query letter. All we need to know is that Marshall solves the problem.
8. What is "it" here? The object is "special truck," but I'm not sure that's what this writer means.
9. I'm surprised that these comps focus on gnomes/leprechauns because the title is so truck-heavy. Trucks are a huge and obvious sales hook in picture book, but the truck almost seems like an afterthought here. This disconnect could be a concern.
10. Already published, or available to submit? This is unclear, and it's an important detail.

PICTURE BOOK QUERY #3 FEEDBACK

THIS IS a long query letter for picture book. And my biggest feedback on it has to do with the concept/story, rather than the query itself. The writer is playing with a few elements: a gnome, mining, a missing truck. From the query, I can't seem to understand how they fit together. I wonder why the focus is the gnome and not the titular truck, because the latter is a much stronger sales hook.

To make the query and overall pitch more compelling, I'd recommend that the writer pare down the query, spend less time on the details, and more time selling the reader on how gnomes and lucky trucks are connected ... and why both are important to the character and plot.

What's the takeaway? There is mention of teamwork, but that theme is not fully connected to the rest of the story. Most strong picture book queries delve into the bigger picture thematic element more. With some focus, I'd love to see this query closer to 200 words.

PICTURE BOOK QUERY #4 (337 WORDS)

THIS PROJECT WAS ALREADY self-published and now the writer wants to submit the series for traditional publication.

DEAR AGENT:

I'm a law professor who has published extensively in my field—and now **I've** written a second children's[1] picture book. I'm hoping that you might be interested in both books.[2]

The first book (about 600 words) was published by an independent publisher in the fall of 2017, and titled XYZ. The book's website is www.(redacted).com. The lead character is a windbag whose highfalutin talk [causes comic scenes with kids who don't understand him][3]. But he finally learns his lesson when a little girl slips off a dock and has to be rescued—fast. [After a year, the book has sold about xxxx copies][4], including sales from school visits, [which have been very successful][5]. You can see photos and reviews on the book's webpage and YouTube channel. (Links[6].)

My contract with the publisher of the first book is flexible: I can cancel with notice. The publisher does not promote the book other than on its website. [The book did recently win a Moonbeam Award][7]. [I have not yet signed a contract for the second book. Again, I'm hoping to find a traditional publisher for both].

The second **manuscript** (about 800 words) is called TITLE. As the title suggests, **the main character** reverts to his fancy-talking ways—again causing funny moments with kids. Among other things, his monkey gets loose and is almost taken by monkeynappers, [but kids come to the rescue][8].

[I'd love to send you both books. I could send a PDF of the first one and the manuscript for the second one. Obviously, I think that people who bought one would want the other][9].

The book grows out of my interest in [plain language (clear communication)][10] in legal and official documents. After 30 years of writing and speaking, and three published law books, [I have an international reputation and following in the field, so there is a ready audience for my work].[11]

Please find both manuscripts (see my suggestion in the margins) copied and pasted below. This is a simultaneous submission. Thank you [for reading this letter and considering my books].[12]

(Signature)

---

1. Omit this. "Children's picture book" is redundant.
2. Be more specific here: "in both the independently published project and its sequel." See more about this in the feedback chapter, which immediately follows this query.
3. This sounds like an adult protagonist in a picture book, which is often problematic. This might send up red flags with an agent or publisher.
4. For all self-published writers, this is a very important lesson: Cite those sales! This is the #1 piece of data that an agent or publisher will want to know as they consider a previously self-published project.
5. A bit of editorializing here that the writer could omit.
6. If the writer has online presence, definitely include links, but consider putting them below the signature instead.
7. A specific year?
8. This does ease my concern about the adult protagonist somewhat, but this approach to character is still unusual in picture book. I'd probably wonder why a kid isn't the central hero who has to clean up after this adult and his foibles.

9. Instead, I would enclose (via copying and pasting) both manuscripts, for the published and unpublished projects. Mention that the fully illustrated PDF for the first project is ready to send upon request. This phrasing makes it sound like the writer doesn't know what to send and is brainstorming. Instead, present what can be sent now (without an attachment) and what else is available.
10. Why say both? Pick one.
11. I'm not sold on this. The picture book audience is not the same as the law book audience. It's great that the writer has a platform and a publishing history, of course. But in this case, they might not convince gatekeepers of the crossover potential.
12. These are similar, for all intents and purposes. The writer could cut one.

PICTURE BOOK QUERY #4 FEEDBACK

THIS QUERY LETTER is unique because it pitches a self-published series. One book from the series has already been published, and the writer is hoping that a publisher scoops the property up in the middle of the series, republishes the first book, and then issues the second one. Make no mistake (and please don't shoot the messenger):

When you self-publish, your book is already published.

Many writers self-publish, mistakenly thinking they're just "trying something" or "taking the market temperature" for their work. But when self-publishing turns out to be more difficult than they anticipated, or they realize how much work is involved in marketing their new project, some decide to approach traditional publishers to "take over." Unfortunately, this is not exactly how things work. The book is already published. It is not a project in progress. There is nothing to take over, since, in a publisher's eyes, the publishing part is already done.

Now, we've all heard of self-published projects that are then picked up by traditional houses and given a new life. *50 Shades of Grey* comes to everyone's mind. Why? Because it's unusual for this to happen. Agents and publishers do sometimes consider already-published projects, but they're usually looking at one thing and one thing only: sales. If a project sells 200 copies independently, that's nice, but it's usually not compelling enough to get a traditional house on board. The publisher will think that all the people who *were* going to buy it (usually folks in the writer's direct network and other low-hanging fruit) have likely already bought it.

That house might not see an opportunity to further amplify the book on the back of demonstrably low demand.

But if you've sold 10,000 copies? In a year? That tells the publisher that the idea and execution themselves have legs, and there's likely a larger, untapped market. Now, the project becomes compelling.

Alas, this is one of the only scenarios where a house would consider coming into a series in the middle. It will cost them money to repackage the books that are already published. It'll be an additional investment to take over any new manuscripts in the pipeline. Is there enough sales potential here?

These submissions are usually decided very quickly, and the existing sales figure is the most important factor, so be sure to include a number, no matter what it is.

The other thing agents and publishers will want to see is platform or marketing reach. In the case of this query, I'm not sold that the writer's law book writing fame will translate to picture book. The markets are simply two separate animals. While the experience is great and tells me that the writer knows what they're doing, the argument that there's crossover appeal doesn't hold a lot of water, realistically.

With self-published queries, the goal is to try. The worst thing that can happen is that the agent or publisher declines. For a query under these circumstances, this writer hits all the major points and provides all of the necessary information. Now it's a question of whether it's enough to convince the agent or publisher past their initial hesitation to take on an already-published project.

PICTURE BOOK QUERY #5 (232 WORDS)

DEAR EDITORS÷,

Big on word play and wit, INTERESTING OKAPI is a humor picture book for [kids ages 5-8 and their adult readers][1]. This 330-word story [features back-and-forth banter reminiscent of Abbott and Costello's infamous "Who's on First" routine][2].

Okapi has an interesting name. He can't wait to tell his new friend Ostrich about it. But Ostrich misunderstands. Entirely. [Ostrich just doesn't get that while Okapi's name might be interesting, his name is definitely not Interesting][3]. Ostrich pulls several interesting facts from Okapi along the way, until Fabulous shows up. In the end, Okapi [considers his new **"Interesting"** nickname might be a good fit after all][4].

Comp titles include Cece Bell's I YAM A DONKEY[5] and BOB, NOT BOB by Liz Garton Scanlon and Audrey Vernick. Both of these stories also feature plots built on linguistic misunderstandings. INTERESTING OKAPI [differs with its resolution of acceptance and its themes of self-respect and friendship][6].

I've been a professional writer for 20 years and have numerous publication credits in the field of healthcare marketing. Picture book manuscripts of mine were selected as finalists in the 2018 and 2016 PNWA Literary Contest. My work has also appeared in regional magazines including *Ohio Magazine, Kentucky Living,* and *Atlanta Parent.* I've received several awards from business writing organizations and am an active member of SCBWI.

The[7] full manuscript is below. This is a simultaneous submission. Thank you for considering my work.

Sincerely,

(Signature)

---

1. This is (about) the age range for picture book, and adults are obviously reading to kids in this category, so the writer doesn't need to mention either. The picture book market veers more toward three-to-seven-year-old readers, actually, so by naming a range that's a bit off, especially an older age range for a shorter (younger-seeming) text, the writer actually brings their market knowledge into question. I'd avoid that altogether and just call it a "picture book." Problem solved!
2. Interesting! Some nice sales hooks here, from this to "big on word play and wit." The market really likes humorous picture books.
3. Ha!
4. Maybe make clear *what* Okapi ends up claiming at the end. With all this talk about names, it's easy to get lost (which is the point of the book, but shouldn't happen in the query).
5. Manuscript titles can be italicized or formatted in caps. Published titles are usually italicized. But there's something to be said for consistency, so use caps throughout.
6. The voice (which has been great so far) dries out a bit here. Maybe try to rephrase, e.g., "brings the fun home with themes of acceptance, self-respect, and friendship." This makes the project sound like it has "humor and heart," which is a market sweet spot.
7. I recommend breaking this logistical stuff into its own paragraph, rather than making it part of the bio. This was originally part of the premise line.

PICTURE BOOK QUERY #5 FEEDBACK

A GREAT PICTURE BOOK PITCH! The writer demonstrates strong focus on their angles. I'd encourage them to play up the "humor with heart" piece when they discuss theme. The only question that remains is whether this writer's agent and publisher targets enjoy wordplay. If they do, then the project will be hitting their sweet spot with this well-crafted query.

This walks the line between being a narrative book (there is clearly a story here) and a concept book (with the comedy routine providing the structure). Concept books tend to be quite hit-or-miss in the market, because if the agent or publisher doesn't like the concept, then they're not going to go for it. But if the writer is doing strong research and finding agents or publishers like picture books with humor, wit, puns, etc., this is going to get close consideration.

PICTURE BOOK QUERY #6 (257 WORDS)

Dear Agent,

I would love for you to consider my 530-word picture book AIR BAND FAMILY. I've been deliberate in not gendering the main character in the manuscript, [and I've also envisioned the musical sounds to be shown as part of the illustrations][1]. [The family is an amalgam of my own family and another one that is dear to my heart][2].

Jesse plays saxophone just like Grammy, who is in a real band. [Grammy'~~s~~ taught Jesse all about what she calls the "music of the soul." But even daily practices haven't earned Jesse an invitation to play in Grammy's band][3]. Instead, Jesse has to settle for lip-synching in the family's air band. Mommy and Mama are on air guitar and big sister is on drums. [Baby **B**rother actually shows some promise on real drums, but Jesse makes him play air triangle to keep Grammy from noticing][4]. Together the family rock out to The Beatles and Nirvana—*Weh-ne-nah Weh-na-na Weh-ne-nah*—until Grammy has to leave for a gig. Maybe tonight is the night that Grammy will finally notice Jesse is ready to join her band[5].

My publishing credits include the self-published middle grade adventure, PIRATE ISLAND, which was the Milford Public Library's 2018

One City, One Story middle grade read; the self-published YA fantasy, ELIXIR BOUND; and poems in *Highlights Hello* magazine. I am also a regular contributor to the Red Tricycle parenting blog (http://redtri.-com/bump-baby) and a PAL member of the SCBWI. To learn more about me please visit my website at www.(redacted).com.

Please find the manuscript pasted below, per your guidelines. Note that this is a simultaneous submission. Thank[6] you so much for your time.

Sincerely,

(Signature)

---

1. Maybe too much detail to put in the query. The writer shouldn't get into prescriptions for the illustrations here. If they are so compelled, they can put this information in an illustration note in the manuscript itself. Consider this article: "Including Illustration Notes In Your Children's Book Manuscript"
2. This personal detail is nice, but I might omit it. The query is, above all, a business letter. If this absolutely must stay in, it should go in the bio paragraph instead, rather than the opening paragraph, which is more suited to logistical information, personalization, and/or the sales hook.
3. Why would Grammy seemingly mentor Jesse but not invite them to play in the band? It seems strange that Grammy would gatekeeper this fun activity in a picture book.
4. I wonder if this makes Jesse a less likeable character. Grammy shutting Jesse out is also a bit suspect (see above). If the whole point is to have fun as a family, why would she keep Jesse from it? The conflict seems like it hinges on one character's whims rather than anything the protagonist can or can't do to change their own fate. This makes me worry that the character won't really be active in the story. I also have concerns about whether the emotional logic will make sense (as the character is struggling with an arbitrary problem).
5. Again, I worry that Jesse is powerless here.
6. The writer might want to consider breaking this out into a separate sign-off paragraph.

PICTURE BOOK QUERY #6 FEEDBACK

THIS IS a fun-sounding picture book idea ... I think. I'm afraid to confess that the conflict doesn't make a lot of sense to me. Grammy seems keen to mentor Jesse but won't let Jesse join the band. And Jesse seems to be trying ("daily practices"). Instead, Jesse jams with their family air band but feels so slighted by Grammy that they sabotage their own baby brother … I think? Again, there's a lot of detail in the query letter itself, but the logic is fuzzy.

This also gives readers two characters who don't come across as especially sympathetic: Grammy herself, and then Jesse, who is forced to act out because of rejection. For the picture book market, this hits a bit of a sour note.

Obviously, this feedback isn't so much a query issue as it is a story consideration. If Grammy and Jesse are actually wonderful and nurturing toward one another, that'd be great to convey in the query. In that case, the emotional logic and story pitch might need to be handled differently. Otherwise, the story sounds fun, but I can't quite understand *why* the obstacle is an obstacle. Maybe part of that can be smoothed over by putting the solution in the query rather than leaving it vague with "Maybe tonight ..."

A happy ending might work well to answer some of these questions. (But if Grammy does finally accept Jesse, I may still be wondering what took her so long and why she was so opposed to it.) It seems the writer is working hard to be inclusive with this project, so this dissonance is especially strange.

PICTURE BOOK QUERY #7 (203 WORDS)

This query is **for an author-illustrator project, where one creator is responsible for both the project's words and illustrations.**

Dear Agent~~,~~

[I hope this letter finds you well][1].

[I'm contacting you to submit for your consideration][2] my picture book manuscript titled STORYTELLER'S HELPER, a 466-word picture book intended for children 2-6 years old[3].

When a traveling storyteller entrusts a curious boy with all of her words, [he becomes inspired to develop his unique voice, and become the teller of his own story][4]. STORYTELLER'S HELPER is a lyrical journey for the senses, **all about** self-discovery~~,~~ and the power of words.

I am an author/illustrator and an active member of SCBWI-MI as well as the Storytellers Academy, ~~studying~~ **where I study** under Jim Averbeck and Arree Chung. My children's book art has been featured twice by the Society of Illustrators NY in their "Original Art" exhibit.

Picture book titles I've illustrated include:

- PLEASE BURY ME IN THE LIBRARY by J. Patrick Lewis (Houghton Mifflin Harcourt)

- I LOVE MY PIRATE PAPA by Laura Leuck (Houghton Mifflin Harcourt)

- ALWAYS LISTEN TO YOUR MOTHER by Florence Parry Heide (Disney Hyperion)[5]

Please take a moment to view my portfolio at www.kylemstoneart.com[6]. Also, I have multiple manuscripts prepared if you'd like to review additional work.

You can find the text pasted below, per your guidelines, and illustration samples and/or a dummy at (URL). Please note that this is a simultaneous submission. Thank you very much for your time and consideration.

Sincerely,

(Signature)

---

1. The writer could honestly dispense with this little pleasantry.
2. Wordy. Avoid the warm-up. We all know why we're here.
3. Quite redundant to mention the category and then the age range. The writer could simply say "picture book" and leave it at that. It's also unclear if this is an author/illustrator project. That would be more helpful to include right up front, as it is a selling point for many agents and publishers, especially from an accomplished illustrator.
4. A good pitch for the story. I might recommend one or two more sentences with specific plot points to describe exactly what happens and how the boy discovers his voice.
5. Some great big publisher experience! I might take this out of bullet points and fold it more naturally into the bio paragraph, however.
6. This writer has opted to reveal their identity in this resource to share their portfolio.

PICTURE BOOK QUERY #7 FEEDBACK

THIS IS a strong query for a picture book, made sweeter by the fact that we're hearing from a published illustrator with an author/illustrator project (an enviable proposition).

Unfortunately, there is very little time spent actually pitching the story. I might want to know a bit more about the character, why finding a voice is important to him, and how he goes about discovering his own self-expression. I also want to know whether he will be proactive, despite getting an assist from the storyteller character. What kind of scenes am I going to see in this story? What will the bulk of the plot entail?

It's very possible that the manuscript or dummy will reveal all if I just scroll down, but a little more summary is a good opportunity to whet the agent or publisher's appetite, so this writer shouldn't skimp.

PICTURE BOOK QUERY #8 (204 WORDS)

DEAR AGENT,

WOLF-DRAGON is a picture book of 1,250[1] words, for ages **six to eight**[2], about self-identity.

Soot and Snow are family, even if one is a dragon and the other, a wolf. [When they are at a Howling, another dragon interrupts their song and makes fun of Soot for acting like a wolf, not a dragon][3]. So Soot sets off to find his inner dragon, teaching himself through trial and error how to breathe fire and fly. But it takes rescuing Snow from the other dragon for Soot to find his flight, and[4] he realizes that no matter how great it is to be a dragon[5], the wolves are still his family.

WOLF-DRAGON will appeal to children who have grown up in adoptive or foster situations, as well as adults and children[6] who would enjoy a fun story about a dragon[7].

In addition to picture books, I also write poetry and adult fiction. My poetry book, TITLE, was published by PUBLISHER. I have also been published in (redacted), and other online journals. One of my poems was the winner of Poetry Contest and was published in TITLE.

Thank you for your time and consideration. **Please note that this is a simultaneous submission.** [The entire manuscript is included below][8]. I look forward to hearing from you.

(Signature)

---

1. The picture book market is heading toward shorter and shorter (and younger!) texts. This project is way over the 600-word upper limit that gatekeepers generally want. This is obviously a potential story issue, not a query issue, but it's something for the writer to take very seriously. Word counts aren't just arbitrary guidelines. Long picture books, in my experience, could usually use some trimming.
2. This is definitely the upper range for picture books, as well. Since this is on the outer fringe of the category, I would keep the audience age range in the query. Usually, my advice is that "picture book" implies an audience of three-to-seven-year-olds and that the writer doesn't need to explain further. Here, though, I'd clarify that the story slants older. The writer should also spell out ages, rather than using numerals.
3. A lot of detail. Queries are meant to be read quickly. Chop this into two sentences. It's all good stuff, but it could be paced more tightly.
4. A good place to break this sentence up.
5. I fully realize that it's tough to pitch a dragon book without saying "dragon" a lot, but this is extreme. Don't reach for a thesaurus, either. The secret is to try rephrasing instead.
6. The writer is saying it will "appeal to children ... and children." This could use some attention.
7. The dragon sales hook (stories about dragons are popular) is obvious. Not sure it needs separate explanation.
8. I'm relocating this from its original spot in the query meat paragraph and making the sign-off its own entity. This order makes more sense to me.

PICTURE BOOK QUERY #8 FEEDBACK

THIS IS A GOOD QUERY. The story is very clearly presented, and themes are woven in well at the end of the pitch. Self-discovery is a rich, universal topic for any children's category, from picture book to young adult.

Since the writer is a poet, is the book going to be in verse? I'd mention whether it's a rhyming text or not somewhere in the query (probably in the manuscript logistics paragraph, next to the title, word count, and audience). This makes a big difference, since some agents and publishers are actively looking for rhyming texts, and others are actively *not*[1]. Picture books in verse tend to be polarizing.

The writing is clear, but the longer sentences could be broken up. The publishing experience in the bio proves the writer has credits. It looks like, even though the titles and publications are redacted for the purposes of this guide, the real query cites specific publishers and contest names appropriately.

For a picture book query, it really can be this simple and short!

My only concern, from a bigger picture perspective, is that word count. Even for the upper age range of the picture book market, this project is long for what publishers are currently doing. Gatekeepers might have a knee-jerk reaction to overcome in this department. But this feedback is offered about a text sight unseen, so it should be taken with a grain of salt.

---

1. Remember the agent who didn't like "verse and vamps" in our Submission Process chapter?

PICTURE BOOK QUERY #9 (185 WORDS)

Dear Ms. / Mr. Agent:

I have written a 500-word, [humorous picture book intended for **four-to-nine-year-olds**][1], titled THE LION CUB THAT BECAME A LITTLE HORSE~~, for your consideration~~[2]. When a frolicking lion cub practices roaring so much that he strains his voice, he misunderstands the meaning of his diagnosis of being "a little hoarse,"~~,~~ [putting him on a jaunty path of redefining who he thinks he's meant to be][3].

Readers will enjoy following this endearing lion cub's hilarious attempt at self-discovery, especially if they are also fans of ~~"~~***The Pout-Pout Fish***~~"~~[4] by Deborah Diesen, and Ross Burach's, ~~"~~***Truck Full of Ducks,***~~"~~ and[5] a similar example of children also learning to listen for clarity and comprehension is ~~"~~***How Much Can a Bare Bear Bear? What Are Homonyms and Homophones?***~~"~~ by Brian P. Cleary. [Repetitive, rollicking rhyme and a bonus 200-word back matter full of fun lion facts with embedded multiple-choice homophones complements this romping adventure, and may give it a crossover appeal to older audiences and fascinate animal lovers of all ages][6].

~~I hope you will find this to be of interest~~[7]. **The complete manuscript is pasted below. Please note that this is a simultaneous submission.** Many thanks for your time and consideration.

Sincerely,

(Signature)

---

1. The picture book target audience here is off. Most picture books are for three-to-seven-year-olds, and that is implied when the writer simply says "picture book." But naming the wrong age range communicates that the writer's market knowledge may not be strong, so I'd avoid it. Do it right, or don't do it at all.
2. As is, the writer is saying that they've "written the book ... for your consideration," which is probably not true. They're "submitting" it for the agent's consideration.
3. Good stuff here, but I'd break this up into two sentences. As a logline, it's quite long. There's no law that says a logline needs to be one sentence, especially if this pressure makes the writer contort themselves into a pretzel.
4. Published titles are italicized rather than put in quotation marks.
5. I'd recommend the writer break this sentence up.
6. This is a very long sentence. Also, is the 200-word back matter part of the word count? I'd pitch one category very strongly (in this case, picture book makes the most sense) rather than trying to create crossover appeal. This project is also straddling fiction and nonfiction with this additional material, and those projects can be a tough sell. Consider this article: "Writing Nonfiction Picture Books"
7. This is implied. The writer could omit it.

PICTURE BOOK QUERY #9 FEEDBACK

THIS STARTS out as a strong picture book query, but then a few elements are added that dilute the pitch. The story seems rather simple, and the writer does a good job of focusing on the wordplay appeal and the theme of identity, which are two strong hooks for this market. But then, later in the pitch, there's a huge sentence that changes my initial concept of the work. (The length of the sentence is also an issue.)

First, I learn that there's educational back matter, which skews the project toward nonfiction. Back matter is less commonly included with fiction. A fiction/nonfiction blend can be tough to pull off, so this may not be the strongest choice. I am totally fine with including fun back matter with lion and sound facts, but maybe the writer shouldn't highlight it so much in the query

Second, the writer attempts to pitch it as a crossover for "animal lovers of all ages." This is problematic. Publishers work in categories, especially in children's books. All marketers know that a "one size fits all" product or book doesn't exist. It's simply not desirable, either, because no publisher can market one thing to *everyone*. Marketing works better when it's specific.

So the writer starts out with a picture book pitch, but then we learn that they actually intend to reach a much larger audience. The problem is, crossover appeal is not manufactured, and it doesn't happen much in picture books because what interests a three-year-old is not going to be the same as what interests a twelve-year-old and what interests a ninety-year-old.

A 200-word blurb of compelling facts isn't going to propel this book onto the general fiction shelf at the bookstore, either. To imply so communicates some naïve expectations about the realities of the publishing marketplace, I'm afraid. The only real crossover picture book with any kind of traction that I can think of is *Oh, the Places You'll Go!* by Dr. Seuss. That's because people love to both read it to kids and buy it for high school and college graduates every June.

This idea, as presented, doesn't strike me as either nonfiction or crossover. So the writer dilutes their own pitch by introducing these ideas, and doing so late in the query. The writer should focus on the story. It's pretty short right now. Is there anything else to add about character, plot, wordplay or theme? There's also a conspicuous lack of bio information here. I'd include at least one sentence. If it doesn't turn into an entire paragraph, the writer can feel free to combine the author portion with the query logistics paragraph at the very end.

Chapter Book Queries

CHAPTER BOOK QUERY #1 (314 WORDS)

Received Representation and a Book Deal!

Dear Agent,

I'm querying based on (current clients, etc.). I hope you will be interested in my chapter book, *The Fairy Dollhouse,* complete at 7,500 words. [Two sisters receive a magical dollhouse which turns them into fairies][1].

Cambria and Lavender Moon receive an old dollhouse from their grandma. When they find rings hidden in the house's cupboard, they put them on and ~~are~~ immediately ~~shrunk down to~~ **turn into** fairies. They land in a life-size version of the house in the middle of a bustling fairy village.

[They discover a beautiful fairy horse standing in the back garden. Suddenly, he coughs a puff of pink bubbles][2].

Cambria and Lavender learn their family[3] operates Moon Manor: Cures for Magical Illnesses. Cambria heads straight for the house's library to see how they can treat the creature[4]. She believes he has

Bubble Trouble Syndrome, which is caused[5] by drinking too much enchanted water. [They find a cough syrup recipe with four ingredients: eucalyptus leaves, peppermint, a spoonful of honey, and a pinch of fairy dust][6].

[Lavender can't wait to see how fast she can fly and to explore the woods on an adventure. Cambria wants to be sure they follow the directions and don't get lost][7].

[The sisters must work together to find the ingredients before nightfall and make a remedy to heal the fairy horse before he gets any worse][8].

The Fairy Dollhouse features a sibling relationship, a dash of magic, [as well as facts about botany and animals][9]. It will appeal to fans of *Sophie the Mouse* series by Poppy Green and *Zoey & Sassafras* by Asia Citro.

I am member of SCBWI and have attended multiple conferences. [Since chapter books are part of a series, I am working on an outline and pages for the second book][10].

(Bio paragraph here.)

Please find the (required number) of pages included per submission guidelines. **This is a multiple submission.** Thank you and have a wonderful day!

(Signature)

---

1. I'd avoid repeating the same idea twice in quick succession (see the underlined portions). Is there a way to compress and streamline?
2. This doesn't seem like enough substance for a standalone paragraph. I'm wondering about the formatting. Also, this is a fun detail but its significance (the coughing horse) isn't clear until later. As is, this seems like set dressing only (though it's not).
3. Their actual family in real life or a parallel version of their family in the fairy world? Be clear about worldbuilding.
4. Put this objective earlier (after the horse coughs) to establish a strong plot driver and draw more attention to it. It's initially unclear that the coughing matters.
5. This will always be a formal, dry word, especially for this age group. I'd avoid it.
6. Too much detail for the purposes of a query.
7. This seems random here. There isn't much of a transition in or out of this paragraph.
8. Good. What are the personal stakes for the sisters, though? Why do they care, other than simply being nice?

9. This seems oddly placed here. Fiction/nonfiction hybrids can be a tough sell. Consider this article (even if written about picture books, the concepts apply here): "Writing Nonfiction Picture Books"
10. Often, but not always. I'd avoid making blanket statements about the market, even though chapter books are, indeed, series-driven. Just say that it has "series potential."

CHAPTER BOOK QUERY #1 FEEDBACK

There are certainly strong elements here. Fairies and ponies and magic and sparkles are attractive for girl readers in the chapter book market. The word count and voice in the query (for the most part, except some redundancy and the very dry "caused") are appropriate for chapter book, so this feels well targeted. But there are some random-seeming transitions which I'd counsel the writer to iron out.

Overall, the story pitch could be tightened, stripped of extra detail, and made more personal. The sisters are thrust into a magical adventure, but the goal of the query is to make them seem like story-driving heroes, instead of simply kids along for the ride. Consider this article:

"Writing a Proactive Protagonist"

The family connection to this realm is also mentioned but not brought full circle, which is a missed opportunity, because it seems like this could tie everything together.

CHAPTER BOOK QUERY #2 (326 WORDS)

Dear Agent,

I am contacting you ~~in regard to~~ **about**[1] my children's chapter book *Transport Captain 42: Crash! Bang! Unicorn Catastrophe!*[2]

Transport Captain 42: Crash! Bang! Unicorn Catastrophe is a~~n~~[3] science fiction action adventure chapter book [that should appeal to young readers][4] who enjoy stories with a female protagonist. It is similar in tone and scope to ~~the graphic novels~~ *Zita the Space Girl* and the *Cleopatra in Space* series[5]. The manuscript is 13,246 words long[6].

Transport Captain 42[7] is the story of an android named 42 and her adventures as the captain of the small transport star ship, **the** Jumpin' Jack, [hauling cargo and taking on odd jobs to pay for the all important fuel needed to continue her voyages][8]. 42 is an ancient piece of technology created by a long-forgotten alien race and knows very little about her origins. [Part of her mysterious construction includes a suite of gadgets and weapons that pop out of her limbs seemingly at random. They're sometimes helpful to the situation at hand, but other times, an embarrassment that she cannot control or disable][9]. She's like a space-age Inspector Gadget [without complete control of her body][10].

Joining her in her adventures is her co-pilot and friend, The Admiral, a dog-like creature with the head of a corgi stuck in a fish bowl, the body of a Koosh Ball, and disembodied limbs that some how propel him without being physically attached to his body. [A host of other colorful characters of various alien races fill out the rest of the story, including the dinosaur-like antagonist Teef Arnell, a big game hunter and poacher of rare and desirable creatures across the galaxy who wants the unicorns that 42 is transporting to their new home on another planet][11].

I am a member of the Society of Children's Book Writers and Illustrators.

The first XYZ pages are pasted below, per your guidelines. Please note that this is a simultaneous submission. Thank you for taking the time to read my query. [I hope to hear from you at your earliest convenience][12].

Sincerely,

(Signature)

---

1. Yes, the query is a business letter, but it's possible to get too formal. "About" works better here.
2. This initial paragraph could use more information. Word count? A short logline? Personalization about why this writer is reaching out to a certain agent or publisher? Or the writer can combine the first and second paragraphs, but then they shouldn't repeat the title in close proximity.
3. Some basic errors here. See the feedback chapter immediately following.
4. Redundant. Chapter books are for young readers. The writer names the category in the above sentence, so this could be omitted.
5. Is the project intended to be a graphic novel? If so, make that part of the initial pitch so the agent or publisher has all the facts. Otherwise, the writer shouldn't use two graphic novels as comp titles. If this is intended as a graphic novel, are the illustrations available? Or is this a text-only submission?
6. The writer can round up instead of citing the precise word count.
7. Try to pitch the story without having to use the title quite so many times.
8. Queries are meant to be read quickly, and this sentence runs long. There's a lot of detail here that the writer can break up.
9. Some dry, wordy construction here. The writer should read this aloud to themselves and see how they might rephrase.
10. This part is clear already. Is all of this detail necessary? I don't care as much about her physical body as I do about how this element fits into the larger story.

11. A ton going on here, but it's not structured intentionally. Instead, this reads like a list. Establish these elements in sequential order. Also, while the writer has clearly made some fun character choices, we're getting all physical description and not much in the way of plot. Ideally, the story will sell the agent or acquiring editor, rather than the quirky visuals (which are a bonus but not the point of the novel).
12. Implied, could omit.

CHAPTER BOOK QUERY #2 FEEDBACK

The writer spends a lot of time on physical description here. I understand that 42 has some visual quirks, and that The Admiral is strange and funny. There is a *lot* of detail here, but the writer never demonstrates how these physical attributes contribute to the story.

Instead, I'd advise this writer to dive into character development and plot. What is 42's emotional journey? Robot stories are tough because one could argue that robots don't have emotions or emotional narrative arcs, unless they're, you know, WALL-E. If there's no character development, that's going to be a huge liability because readers in the chapter book category want to bond with characters, above all.

So what is 42's story? What does she need to learn about herself or accomplish to make herself whole? Don't let her physical appearance stand in for true characterization. Readers (including agents and publishers) will want more substance.

Right now, the plot is crammed into one sentence at the very end of the query meat and completely stops the forward momentum of the pitch. The writer introduces the antagonist, the stakes, and something seemingly important that 42 is doing—all in one fell swoop. Woof. I feel like I've been hit by a train. These things are crucial. The writer should slow down and take some time with them. Give gatekeepers more plot points, not just a summary list. Consider this article:

"Query Letter Plot Pitch: Premise vs Plot"

Finally, this query has a weakness that's a deal-breaker. There are some proofreading errors, including article, hyphenation, and punctuation mistakes. There is also some wordiness that gets in the way of both reading comprehension and reading pleasure. Queries are meant to be read quickly. I'm not asking for choppy sentence fragments, but this writer would do well to read their work aloud and see where they run out of breath. That's always an indicator of an overwritten sentence.

The writer doesn't want their work to be, well, *work* to read. Nobody likes to hear this, but a basic grammatical error in the query can stop a pitch cold. The English language is the writer's only tool, and if they're making a fundamental mistake, they are are not going to convince anyone to give them a writing job (which is what they're seeking here). Proofread, proofread, proofread! If this writer still finds themselves coming up short, they can ask someone else to be a second set of eyes on this important document.

CHAPTER BOOK QUERY #3 (175 WORDS)

DATE

Agent name and agency name

Re: TITLE, an original fairy tale in chapters (5,000 words)[1]

Dear Agent,

[Character is deathly ill. His daughters undertake a great adventure to obtain the cure he needs. Well, one of them does][2]. [TITLE is a quest story filled with adventure, danger, magic, deceit, honesty, just a tinge of romance,][3] [and geese. Lots of geese][4].

I am sending this to you because (how my work matches your wish list/current needs).

I take classes at the Loft Literary Center in Minneapolis, MN and have studied with such teaching artists as Molly Beth Griffin, Allison McGhee, Anika Fajardo, and Morgan Grayce Willow. My fiction and nonfiction works have appeared in various magazines including *Northwoods Woman* and *DONA International*[5] and in the anthology, *Talking Stick*. I was selected by the Newbery Award-winning author Marion Dane Bauer for the Loft's Shabo Award for my picture book manuscript, *Fuzzy Buzzy Bumble Bee*[6]. I also received Honorable Mention for my children's story, *Codie's Gift*, from the Alabama Writer's Conclave.[7]

As requested[8], XYZ pages of my manuscript are pasted below. **Please note that this is a simultaneous submission.** Thank you, in advance, for your time and consideration.

Sincerely,

(Signature)

---

1. I like seeing the email subject line. Here, I'd add the category of "chapter book" (or "chapter book fairy tale") instead of "in chapters" because the latter is not an accepted term.
2. This story seems to feature an adult character and potentially adult daughters (their ages are not specified). But the project is 5,000 words. That's not nearly long enough for adult readers. An agent or publisher is likely not looking for short stories to represent, unless they're explicitly trafficking in this category. The word count is fitting for a chapter book, but those need to feature child characters. This audience/category confusion is probably the project's biggest liability.
3. I'd take a complete second look at the plot pitch. This is just a list, and the writer needs to make a more compelling case for the story itself. Especially since the main character is not defined here, and the category is unclear. See the feedback chapter immediately following this query.
4. Funny voice! However, I have no idea what this has to do with anything. The geese never come back into the query.
5. Format magazine names, TV shows, movies, published book titles, etc., in italics.
6. Is this project published already or not? Sometimes manuscripts can receive awards, but it's more common to see a published book with an accolade.
7. The bio is rather long compared to the pitch itself.
8. This phrasing makes it seem like the agent or publisher reached out and requested the manuscript. If this is a cold submission, "Per your guidelines," or similar, is more accurate.

CHAPTER BOOK QUERY #3 FEEDBACK

THIS IS GOING to be more story/concept feedback than query feedback, but I do want to really make clear that choosing the right category—and writing something the market recognizes as belonging to that category—is an important part of the submission process. Here, we have adult characters (the daughters' ages aren't specified but the king is obviously a grown-up, there's also a mention of "romance"), and a very short word count.

At 5,000 words, this is either a short story or a chapter book. Those are the two existing publishing buckets for this manuscript length. This writer can either retarget their category, expand the story, or find a different route to market that isn't agent- or publisher-dependent.

Unfortunately, agents don't typically take short stories or fairy tales. That's literary magazine territory, and unless you're an existing client gunning for *The Paris Review*, an agent won't really submit to journals on a writer's behalf.

The argument could be made that this is a picture book in the "illustrated storybook" category, but this bucket doesn't really exist in today's publishing landscape. The "storybook" category used to be a market force and tolerate these higher word counts. This is where fairy tales usually lived. Alas, this market is largely inactive.

That leaves chapter book as an available option, due to the project's low word count and the mention that this is a story "in chapters." But chapter books feature child protagonists almost exclusively. There's also no romance.

There is little information about the adult king and whether he's the main character or not. Some drama is alluded to with the daughters, where only one of them is helpful, but there's no further context for this. I don't know their ages and whether this is their story or the king's.

The writer's bio indicates an interest in children's books, but it's unclear whether this is one. If it *is* a chapter book, it's a chapter book in word count only. From a query standpoint, the plot feels quite thin, as presented, and doesn't reflect the story in a compelling way.

I'm still not sure where the geese come in, either, which raises a question of tone. There's a reason that I'm harping on these geese, I swear! Is this a humorous or absurdist piece? But the query speaks of serious issues, like betrayal.

I'd flesh out the query meat out into at least one or two big paragraphs about the story itself, told in sequential order. Consider this article:

"Query Letter Plot Pitch: Premise vs Plot"

The writer should also mention character ages and arcs. Is this a chapter book or not? If it's a short story for the general literary fiction market, this brings me right back to the obstacle that most agents don't want short stories outside of the occasional collection. This could be a query sent to a literary magazine, of course, but the "in chapters" designation continues to throw me.

Middle Grade Queries

MIDDLE GRADE QUERY #1 (248 WORDS)

RECEIVED REPRESENTATION AND A BOOK DEAL!

DEAR AGENT,

The summer of her tenth birthday, budding lawyer[1] Guinevere St. Clair moves to her parent's childhood home in Sioux, Iowa. It's a fresh start for a family**, which** [has survived a tragedy that left Gwyn's mother, Vienna, unable to remember her husband and two children][2]. Gwyn's science-obsessed father believes that Sioux will be the miracle that brings back his beloved wife's lost memories.

As for Gwyn?[3] Well, she's looking for a case with a more reliable outcome. Barely settled in corn country[4], Gwyn and her little sister, Bitty, <u>meet</u> the formidable Gaysie Cutter[5].

~~On~~ **At** their first <u>meeting</u>[6], Gwyn, a self-described "excellent judge of guilt, innocence, and all verdicts in-between, thank you very much," comes to believe that Gaysie is not only a bad egg, [but a potential murderer][7]. When Gaysie's only friend, Wilbur Truesdale, goes missing, Gwyn becomes amateur sleuth[8], desperate to solve the case by bringing Wilbur home alive~~–and~~[9]**. She must be** daring enough to follow the most dangerous of **clues—even**[10] [if they come from the unreliable mind of her mother][11]. [Gwyn doesn't realize that what she's really looking for is something to make her believe in miracles, too.

A BOAT AGAINST THE CURRENT is a 70,000-word MG novel about a girl trying to understand the brain vs. the heart and reconciling science vs. faith][12]. It may appeal to fans of Sharon Creech's WALK TWO MOONS and Alan Bradley's Flavia de Luce books[13].

Below is the first chapter and I am happy to send more upon request. **Please note that this is a simultaneous submission.**

Thank you,

(Signature)

---

1. Good. Use any opportunity to inject detail, even if it's subtle, like this.
2. Wow! This is an emotional premise right away.
3. It's a good idea to bring focus back to the kid, as Dad seems like the driving force of the story so far, which is a liability in middle grade.
4. Love the phrasing of "corn country" but the move to Iowa is already established.
5. I'd maybe add a bit more detail here instead of simply introducing or naming the character.
6. Avoid word repetition. See the underlined instances and rephrase.
7. This takes a bit of a left turn. How so? The project doesn't seem like a murder story from the set-up, so I'd love some clarification here.
8. Is she a budding lawyer or an amateur sleuth? The two are related but not the same. Streamline the pitch.
9. I suggest breaking this sentence up, as shown.
10. Use an em-dash here.
11. This is important and brings the family element back. Don't "bury the lede" (hide the good stuff) at the end of a longer sentence.
12. A lot of thematic description here. I'd consider streamlining.
13. Perhaps a moot point, but it's important to note that this comp is for adult readers, even if it features a young character. It isn't middle grade. When the writer uses a comp outside of their project's primary category, they need to be sure they know what they're doing and have a compelling reason for it.

MIDDLE GRADE QUERY #1 FEEDBACK

A really nice query and, obviously, this was a success because the book was published under the title *The Unforgettable Guinevere St. Clair* by Atheneum Books. The only thing I would've changed is this shift that happens in the middle, from describing Gwyn's move and family context … to meeting a new character ... to suddenly stumbling across a missing kid and a potential murder. The problem is, these latter two developments seem to affect Gaysie, leaving Gwyn to go along for the ride, rather than drive the bus.

I found this sudden Gaysie focus abrupt without a transition. If the story "takes a turn," the writer will maybe want to tie these various elements together so that the query comes across as cohesive. The bio paragraph is also missing in this letter. This writer clearly didn't need writing clips or relevant experience to get published, but I always like to know a bit about the person behind the pitch.

MIDDLE GRADE QUERY #2 (298 WORDS)

Dear Agent,

Since winning a science contest, [twelve-year old BOBBY LANCASTER[1] has been chased by a Russian mobster, a brother/sister assassin team, and the CIA][2]. Good thing for Bobby, he has a dog like CHARLIE to help him out.

[Charlie, a golden retriever from Beijing, was born in the Year of the Dog][3]. A reverse[4] in nature equipped him with the cognitive and motor skills of humans. Trained in the arts of espionage and kung fu since he was a pup, Charlie was a covert operative for the Chinese government until he escaped to America in hopes of giving up his secret agent life. But with Bobby in trouble, [Charlie won't hesitate to use his special skills, even if it means breaking all eighty-eight of his sacred spy rules to do it][5].

[From Russia to Washington, D.C., as the bad guys close in on Bobby, Charlie is closing in on them][6].

YEAR OF THE DOG is a 60,000-word action-packed story that combines ~~the~~ martial arts and espionage while highlighting the strong bond between a boy and his dog, [and the unique friendships boys have when they're twelve][7].

I have practiced Kung Fu[8] for the last thirty years and have taught it professionally since 1996. I speak in area schools and appear regularly on local television and radio to discuss children's safety. In my writing world, I am the president of a local writers group. [I have short stories published in local anthologies, articles in martial arts magazines, won several honorable mentions in contests, and wrote the screenplay for a tai chi video that sells nationally][9]. YEAR OF THE DOG is a stand-alone with series potential.

(Agent), it would be an honor to work with you. **The first XYZ pages are pasted below. Please note that this is a simultaneous submission**. Thank you for considering YEAR OF THE DOG. I look forward to your reply.

(Signature)

---

1. Don't use all caps formatting for character names. This is expected in a synopsis (for the first mention of that character) but not in a query.
2. This certainly promises high, high stakes, but it's a list. It doesn't give me a sense of the actual order of the plot—or *why* these things are happening. Given that the CIA and Russian mob don't often target twelve-year-olds, this question will come up and could be pre-empted.
3. A strange transition. I'm still wondering about the CIA, and yet I'm being forced to focus on the dog (the lowest stakes element presented so far).
4. Not sure what this term means, given that it suggests *big* changes for the dog. Is it nature? Seems extreme for nature. Or is it more? If this suggests a fantasy/magical element, that needs to be clear.
5. The story seems like it's going to be told from Charlie's POV. He's very much presented as the protagonist here, with big emotional stakes and decisions to make. Whose eyes will the novel be seen through?
6. A great high-stakes hook.
7. This sounds a bit too vague and could be omitted. This also tells me that Bobby will be the POV character. But then why is the entire query meat section told in Charlie's perspective? Is it dual POV? The writer should specify.
8. The writer capitalizes this here, but not above. Pick one and standardize the choice, whatever it is.
9. Cite some titles and publications here. If the writer has professional credits, the agent or publisher may want to look into them, and this doesn't let them do that.

MIDDLE GRADE QUERY #2 FEEDBACK

THIS WOULD BE a strong and compelling query, if only I knew who the protagonist was.

The query starts with Bobby, even giving some details about him. It makes me think that, since Bobby is in danger, this is Bobby's story. Then we shift entirely into Charlie's perspective, and he has some very compelling moral and emotional issues to deal with. Surely, that makes him our protagonist. But then we're back to Bobby.

Unless the novel is also told in Charlie's POV, or Charlie's POV alone, it doesn't make sense to "give" so much of the query to him. If this writer is using a unique narrative choice or structure, such as dual POV, they should highlight that right off the bat.

The list at the beginning of the query also replaces a sequential description of what the plot will actually entail. Consider this article:

"Query Letter Plot Pitch: Premise vs Plot"

Finally, if the writer has professional publishing credits, like the anthologies, magazines, and contest wins, they should cite the relevant names and years to make them sound legitimate. Otherwise, vague references to publication credits or contest honors don't lend these claims as much credibility.

MIDDLE GRADE QUERY #3 / SCI-FI (282 WORDS)

Dear Agent,

[Mortimer grew up on a tiny family spaceship, listening to stories about the wonders of school. Now it's finally time for him to enroll and make his parents proud][1]. He is sent to stay with his great aunt in a huge, hollow asteroid. It's supposed to be paradise~~—a place which combines~~ **combining** the best of space travel with the beauty of nature. [Mortimer finds it utterly terrifying][2], and school also turns out to be far [more stressful than he was led to believe][3].

Mai wants to travel the solar system as a concert **pianist—if**[4] she can just get over her space sickness. On the surface, she seems like a model student, [but she has a dangerous secret—an illegal self-enhancement device **that** helps her maintain her star status][5]. [The last thing she needs is a clueless new boy ~~poking his nose in and~~ wanting to be friends.

Once Mortimer finds his way into Mai's inner circle][6], he wants to use her secret[7] to overcome his phobias and be the son his parents expect. But Mai's device is illegal for good reason, and Mortimer's plans [put more than ~~mere~~ **her** reputation~~s~~ at risk][8].

TITLE, complete at 44,000[9] words, is an MG science fiction story [featuring interfering robots, zero gravity sports][10], and a very fine cat. It will appeal to readers of *The Wild Robot* series by Peter Brown and anything by Frank Cottrell Boyce.

I have been a fan of science fiction since I first read *A Wrinkle in Time* at the age of seven. I currently work as a teaching assistant at a primary school in XYZ, and I'm a member of SCBWI.

Please find the first ABC pages below, per your guidelines. Note that this is a simultaneous submission. Thank you for your time and consideration.

(Signature)

---

1. Good opening. This sets up a compelling and relatable conflict for the character. He is potentially lonely and feels left out. Big changes are coming. Thematically, this is perfect for middle grade.
2. A strong reaction, but no context for it. Why? If the reason is compelling, I'm more likely to care and relate. As is, this seems to be his big conflict, but it's not really specific.
3. How? Is he having trouble fitting in? Does he not know what to do around other kids? Etc. Clarify.
4. I'd use a series of em-dashes here.
5. Very high stakes. The danger of "losing it all" is always compelling.
6. The ideas here are directly contradictory. She does *not* want him as a friend in one sentence. The next, he's in her inner circle. I might consider more of a transition here so that this isn't confusing.
7. He wants to use "the fact that she has a secret" or he wants to use the secret device itself? This phrasing is unclear.
8. This sounds compelling, but I'd be more overt. This phrasing minimizes the potential risk. Why? The writer should work to *maximize* it. Put the very real stakes on the page rather than implying them.
9. It's important to note that this is now considered on the short side for middle grade with sci-fi or fantasy elements. Those range up to about 60,000 words, and maybe more.
10. If you get nothing else from this volume, dear reader, I want to sell the world on the idea that lists are not as compelling as people think they are! This doesn't tell me much of anything about the plot, even if it's mildly amusing.

MIDDLE GRADE QUERY #3 FEEDBACK

A GREAT EXAMPLE OF TWO CHARACTERS' stories woven into one query. The stakes are high, I think, but right now, they're hinted at, rather than fully developed. Go there. The query is not the place to hold back. One other thing to clarify would be whether the novel itself is going to be dual POV on Mortimer and Mai, or if we're just seeing one perspective.

The two-character presentation makes me think dual POV, but every time a writer uses a specific narrative style that's more than just first person or third person and one character, it's worth nothing that right up front in the query, for example, "Told in alternating dual POV chapters, TITLE ..." or similar.

MIDDLE GRADE QUERY #4 / FANTASY (240 WORDS)

DEAR AGENT,

In my middle grade fantasy novel, *Weavers of the Great Light Way: The Awakening*, [Hildy Spinner is a rebellious foster girl who longs to be an aerial acrobat][1]. Her dream of flying becomes a reality when a secret intergalactic school, known as the Order of Weavers, recruits her to find [the Statue of Liberty (she's missing!) before bizarre storms demolish New York City][2].

Turns out a sinister shape-shifter named Belphegore is [destroying Earth's only connection with her cosmic family in his quest to trap humans in fear][3]. [Hildy and her friends must harness the Laws of the Universe, as well as their own power to create][4], before Lady Liberty[5], [and all of Earth's freedoms, are lost forever][6].

At approximately 59,000 words, my novel will appeal to fans of *Wildwood* and *The Girl Who Drank the Moon*. (Personalization about the agent or publisher.)[7]

I'm a writer, producer and script supervisor for feature films and commercials. I'm an active member of SCBWI, as well as a mentorship winner in the 2017 Rutgers University Council on Children's Literature. I've been a finalist in the Page International Screenwriting Awards and a semi-finalist in the Scriptapalooza Screenplay Competition.

Thank you for considering *Weavers of the Great Light Way: The Awakening*. **The first XYZ pages are pasted below, per your guidelines.** Please note this is a simultaneous submission. I hope to hear from you soon.

Warm regards,

(Signature)

---

1. Queries are meant to be read quickly. I'd separate the logistical details (category, title, word count, genre, etc.) from the beginning of the pitch. Here, the writer should clarify why Hildy has this dream, specifically. The desire itself is attention-catching, for sure, but I'm missing a specific personal element that connects it to stakes and character.
2. Ha! This is an attention-catching intro to the story world. Consider me intrigued. I do wonder what this has to do with aerial acrobats, though, and whether NYC is her home or if Hildy travels there on a mission.
3. This sounds good, but I have no idea what it actually means, or how this relates to storms or kidnapping (?) the Statue of Liberty, alas. For all of the fantasy world-building to make sense, it needs a strong sense of logic. How does this antagonist relate to all the stuff that's happening, and how does the stuff serve the antagonist's objective, as described here? Also, does the writer mean "Earth's cosmic family" when referring to "her" or "Hildy's cosmic family"? This could change the meaning of the pitch considerably.
4. This opens up big worldbuilding questions. Writers have to be very specific when pitching fantasy. See the following feedback chapter for more detail.
5. So this is symbolic? It seems a bit overt here, as this is an obvious representation of freedom.
6. Be more specific about stakes. Freedoms like what? How does exterminating freedom serve Belphegore's desire? I'm still stuck on whether I'm understanding how the "cosmic family" fits into all of this.
7. This logistical paragraph is also a perfectly fine place to put personalization. The first paragraph is probably more common, but that doesn't make this option wrong.

MIDDLE GRADE QUERY #4 FEEDBACK

THIS IS a strong query in terms of the writing and mechanics, but it misses on worldbuilding. For fantasy, the worldbuilding is the most important part of the pitch. Fantasy is a crowded market, and the more specific and compelling the logic of the world or magic, the stronger a project's chances of attracting attention.

That's what agents and editors will consider first and foremost, so it bears further definition. The writer mentions, "Hildy and her friends must harness the Laws of the Universe, as well as their own power to create ..." and this throws me.

First of all, the antagonizing action seems pretty recent (NYC was just attacked), but apparently there's already been a whole school established to combat the forces of evil. And maybe some kind of fantasy order. What is the Order of the Weavers? How does it fit into the story?

Make the antagonizing logic very clear, and do the same for the heroic logic. Whenever an agent or publisher gets a pitch for a fantasy, they will want to know what the fantasy elements are and why they're unique in a crowded market. Here, we have the Laws of the Universe (not defined), and "their own power to create" (which sounds nice but is not defined). Does the writer mean actual powers (like the ability to bend matter or fly), or more holistic powers that have looser boundaries (like creativity itself)?

We also have the Order of the Weavers (not defined) and an intergalactic school (which introduces the potential for sci-fi, not just fantasy). We also get mention of a "cosmic family," but it's unclear whose it is—Earth's, Belphegore's, or Hildy's. That is a lot.

And while I know what all the words mean, I don't know how these elements function in this particular story because there isn't specific context yet that ties these ideas together.

The writer also mentions this interesting aerial acrobat element at the very beginning, but it never comes up again. Sure, it's attention-catching, but ideally the ideas from the top of the query end up coming full circle by the end (or are at least woven in somewhere).

MIDDLE GRADE QUERY #5 / HISTORICAL (487 WORDS)

(NAME) MG HISTORICAL Fiction

Approx. 50,000 words

(Date)[1]

Dear Nicole,

[Thank you for this opportunity to submit a query for my][2] MG historical fiction, *Fair Investigations,* complete at 50,000 words. I read your interview on the "Mixed Up Files" blog today, [and noticed you are open to MG and historicals, and love the Brontës. My favorite is *Jane Eyre*][3].

Henry and his sister Alice are on their way to the World Columbian Exposition in 1893, [but more than the enormity and awesomeness of the exhibits awaits them][4]. [Mistaken identities, a trail of clues,[5] and family secrets combine to make this their best adventure yet, weaving mystery and adventure together with a thread of humor][6].

[Disillusioned after losing first place due to a sabotaged physics project, Henry is finished with scientific investigations—or so he thinks][7]. When Henry thwarts a pickpocket and is mistaken for the thief, [his journey becomes one of self-discovery and regained confidence][8] as he applies his once-abandoned[9] scientific skills of deduction to interpret a trail of mysterious clues. They eventually absolve Henry of the crime, leading him to cross paths with his inventor hero, Thomas Edison, **and** placing him on an unimaginable course for a bright future.

Aside from the Richard Peck books of the early 2000s, novels set in the magical and rich setting of the Columbian Exposition have been left unexplored. Like *The Sixty-Eight Rooms* **a**dventure **s**eries[10] (Malone, Vol. 4/2015) and *The Calder Game*[11] (Balliett, 2010), *Fair Investigations* will lead readers through the maze of exhibits, rides and exotic cultural venues never before seen in the 19th century, [much like our internet does today][12].

Fair Investigations fits well with the common core requirements, which focus on physical science investigations and reasoning (**fifth** grade), and industrial revolution/**s**tate history/1877-1914 (**sixth**[13] grade). [A plethora of projects can be based on the thousands of inventions and displays found at the Exposition. Understanding the controversy surrounding Columbus, this story does not focus on the explorer, but on the advancement of technology since the discovery of America. The book will include an author's note explaining such][14].

[Having a degree in education and library/media, and a love for travel and history, I enjoy][15] writing about historical events and the childhood of **lesser-known**[16] figures. [I find inspiration and quirky bits of history when I travel, which inevitably end up on my blog or social media][17]. My publications include articles in *Old Schoolhouse* and *Thriving Family* magazines. I am a member of SCBWI, Word Weavers and ACFW, and am enrolled in an advanced course with the Institute of Children's Literature. My passion is to make Scripture and history come alive for my readers [and **I** strive to make my manuscripts shine][18]. I have won **first** place in **two** writing contests for my MG Historical Fiction, [one of which][19], *The Heart Changer*, debuts in Spring 2019 with Ambassador International.

Please note that this is a simultaneous submission. [Thank you for your careful consideration of this query][20] for my MG historical novel, *Fair Investigations*. The first five pages are pasted below.

Sincerely,

(Signature)

---

1. These are holdovers from letter formatting. This writer probably doesn't need to get quite so elaborate.
2. This is perhaps a bit too earnest. There's a fine line between professionalism and flattery in a query.
3. Compelling personalization!
4. Saying something simple in a complicated way. Try to be more direct.
5. A serial comma is important here.
6. This doesn't tell me much of anything.
7. I'd much rather have the writer begin here after introducing the historical setting.
8. The voice suddenly dries out as the writer starts to analyze the work. Is there room to mention themes later?
9. Already established. No need to repeat.
10. No need to capitalize "adventure series."
11. Published titles should be formatted in italics, not quotation marks.
12. This seems like a random connection. I'd maybe reconsider.
13. Spell these out.
14. While I think this is an important conversation, I don't know if this level of detail is necessary for the purpose of the query. Keep the focus on the sales pitch (the curriculum tie-ins) rather than potential controversy. Or at least streamline this explanation. This writer shouldn't be creating an objection in the gatekeeper's mind while trying to pre-empt an objection, but this might be the unintended consequence of this paragraph.
15. The writer takes too long to get to the subject of this sentence. Rephrase, favoring shorter declarative sentences.
16. Hyphenate.
17. The bio could be tightened.
18. This ideally goes without saying and could be omitted.
19. The writer should refer to specific manuscripts or contests. There's some messy phrasing here. I'd encourage the writer to read this aloud and play with it.
20. This seems a bit like the writer is micromanaging, and as if they assume the agent or publisher won't read carefully. Is that the right tone to set?

MIDDLE GRADE QUERY #5 FEEDBACK

THIS QUERY DOES a good job of selling me on the historical setting. Historical novels tend to be tough to market, unless they have timeliness hooks (an upcoming anniversary, for example), sales hooks (the curriculum tie-ins here are a great example), or explore underrepresented areas of history (this query's setting seems to do this as well). It's great to focus on why this historical stands apart.

That being said, I'm a bit fuzzy on plot and character arc. Here, Henry abandons science but comes back to it. He's set up for a bright future. But other than that, I don't really learn much about him. His struggles, his objectives, how he changes over the course of the story, etc. If he "returns" to his love of science, for example, that means he had it already, and didn't discover it anew.

Instead, Henry might have more of a growth arc for his engagement with science as a result of the plot, and developing the story in this direction could be add stakes as well. It's not that he's "getting his groove back," it's that his eyes are opened to a new world. This point might be more marketable.

Rather than thematic analysis of the themes in the first paragraph, this writer could be more specific about how these things apply to character. Same with plot. The writer falls into two traps here, as do a lot of queries in this guide. Consider these articles:

"Concrete Writing: Using Specific Language"

"Query Letter Plot Pitch: Premise vs Plot"

MIDDLE GRADE QUERY #6 (432 WORDS)

Dear Wonderful Agent,

[Everyone has secrets][1]. Twelve-year-old Willow isn't sure keeping Gram's from Mom and Uncle Quinn is a good idea. [If she stays silent, she'll cheat herself out of a branch of the family her grandmother left behind decades ago][2]. If she speaks up, Mom and Uncle Quinn may never forgive her[3]. BALANCING ACT[4] is a **48,000-word mi**ddle grade[5]. This is a simultaneous submission. I attended the 2016 SCBWI OREGON BETWEEN THE PAGES[6] conference and include 25 pages **pasted below,** per conference guideline. Thank you for this opportunity to share my work.

Willow's grandmother needs some help after breaking her ankle. Mom volunteers Willow for the job. It's a good thing because Auntie Eve, who has been taking care of Gram, [has the empathy of a rock-crusher][7]. Willow abandons her vacation plans to take care of Gram but feels cheated. [This is the first year she's old enough to stay home on her own and she and her best friend have][8] plans[9].

They are both Middle School[10] gymnasts. Willow has perfect balance and is the star of her team but always looking for new tricks ~~to learn~~. When Gram says she knows someone to teach her some tumbling,

Willow jumps at the chance. Johnny arrives the next day. He's young and fit and the grandson of Gram's childhood friend. Or at least that's what he tells her.

Then Willow discovers Gram walked away from the Damele Family Circus when she was sixteen. Johnny is her great-nephew and wants to reunite the family. [Gram never told her own children about her past and doesn't know how to claim her old family after all these years when her new one doesn't know they exist][11]. Willow hatches a plan to help Gram reveal her secret. ~~Willow's~~ Auntie Eve becomes suspicious of Johnny ~~when she drops in to check on Gram~~. She forbids Willow from seeing him.

Everything blows up when Johnny drives Gram and Willow to reunite with his grandmother ~~to settle a decades old misunderstanding~~. Auntie Eve arrives at Gram's empty house and calls the police. Johnny is served with a restraining order. Auntie Eve arranges to ship Gram to a rehab center ~~to recuperate~~ and prepares to send Willow home. Willow teeters between telling her about Gram's past and keeping Gram's secret. [What she does next will determine her future or undermine Gram's past][12].

I am a member of SCBWI, Central Oregon Writers Guild (COWG), and E-Z Writers critique. I served as the preliminary judging coordinator for COWG's annual fourth grade book writing contest from 2009 to 2014, and currently serve as the featured reader coordinator[13].

Sincerely,

(Signature)

---

1. This sounds great, but it could be said of anyone, in any story. I'd actually prefer a more specific opening, e.g. "... Willow isn't sure that keeping Gram's secrets ..."
2. This also dances around what the secret actually is. Be clear. For example, "It turns out Gram has a secret other family!" (Or whatever the case is.)
3. Why? She sounds like a kid put in a tough situation. Why would the adults be vindictive about it rather than understanding?
4. The whole rest of this paragraph really belongs at the end of the query, not at the beginning. This is the writer's sign-off. They can put book logistics (title and word

count) here, but the query logistics portion (what's included, thanking the agent, etc.) always belongs at the end.

5. Hyphenate the word count and don't capitalize the category (middle grade).
6. Capitalize this but don't put it in caps.
7. Ha! Good voice.
8. This sentence doesn't really add much to "feels cheated," so I'd probably omit. This query is longer, as is, so any small cuts the writer can make will help.
9. Avoid word repetition in close proximity. See the underlined instances and rephrase.
10. "Middle grade," "middle school," "high school," "sophomore," etc. are not typically capitalized.
11. Good stuff but an overlong sentence. I'd try to break this up.
12. This sounds nice and dramatic, but it restates the conflict, which is already clear.
13. Put the sign-off information after this paragraph.

MIDDLE GRADE QUERY #6 FEEDBACK

On its face, this is a strong query. It is cleanly written, has glimmers of voice, and portrays a high-stakes situation that could rip a family apart. The perfect cocktail of intergenerational drama and emotion for middle grade (which usually deals more with family as a central theme). Right? Well, yes.

But one crucial element is almost entirely missing. Notice that Willow isn't given much of a story here. She likes gymnastics, which is fine and good, but that's just an interest, not a plot.

Instead, she is thrust into the heart of some big drama by other characters and is left with an impossible decision to make (which shouldn't be a kid's place, anyway). She faces an old conflict between adult characters who shouldn't be putting her in that situation in the first place. She already feels neglected when she loses her summer, and now a bunch of adults are dumping all over her. This is Grandma's family intrigue, and Willow is just along for the ride. That does not, alas, set us up for a strong Willow-driven story. (It's also significant to point out that it seems like most of the tension happened in the past—the present is more about dealing with its ramifications. It's stronger and more immediate for a middle grade story to happen primarily in the now instead.)

This is obviously a potential premise issue, not a query issue. But I am wary of characters who appear passive in a query, like they are crash test dummies strapped into someone else's crazy train. Here, Grandma probably has the meatiest character arc in terms of healing, redemption, and development. Willow, on the other hand, is simply between a rock and a hard place in a situation that she didn't ask for.

To me, the protagonist is whoever changes the most in a story. Here, that's not Willow, and I worry whether she is strong and proactive enough to carry a novel, rather than simply reacting to a big situation that seems entirely out of her hands.

The latter type of story (especially if the situation involves adult drama) doesn't tend to play well in the children's market. Obviously, I'm commenting on the premise, sight unseen, which is always dangerous. But this is the strong impression I get from reading this query, and I worry that agents and publishers may walk away with the same idea.

Willow must be proactive (as much as is possible for her age) and the conflict must center on her. Otherwise, this might not be her story, nor a true middle grade novel.

MIDDLE GRADE QUERY #7 (343 WORDS)

Received Representation!

Dear Andrea,

When I read that you had returned to Transatlantic as an agent, I did a happy dance. I've been looking for an agent since I finished my middle grade novel, *The Wonder List,* and I'm crossing my fingers that you might want to read it. [You mention in your wish list that you're interested in "cathartic" middle grade novels and stories that make you laugh out loud, so I immediately thought of you][1].

Eleven-year-old Dani has a lot of things on her "Wonder List," [big questions that you can't simply plug into a computer][2]—about God and heaven and what it means to be a good person. When she learns that her new friend Naomi is a **born-again**[3] Christian, she decides she'd better become one, too—and fast—if she wants to be "saved." [Besides, it sounds like a really great makeover][4].

There's a lot Dani wishes she could change. Her sister, who suffers from depression, is home from college and occupying her parents' attention. Dani misses her dog walking business and her grandfather, [who they left behind in Pennsylvania][5]. Plus, there's a group of mean girls at her new school—The Princess Charmings—who won't stop teasing her. [Through a series of mishaps that put Naomi and Dani at odds with ~~each other~~ **one another**, Dani learns some valuable lessons about family, friendship, and the importance of being true to yourself][6].

You know my publishing history, so I won't go into a lot of detail. After being in the business for ten years, I got a Masters in Education from Fairfield University and taught eighth-grade English for a short time. I've also written a children's opera based on *Rumpelstiltskin,* which was performed in New York City a few years ago, and am currently freelance editing and writing[7].

[Let me know if you'd like to read a partial or full manuscript][8]. [I also have several completed picture book texts, so I'd love to know if and when you might be open to those submissions][9].

Thanks, Andrea. I look forward to hearing from you.

Best wishes,

(Signature)

---

1. Great! The query starts out quite familiar and chatty, so I was wondering if the writer had concrete reasons for favoring this particular agent. The writer delivered with specifics!
2. Great definition of "Wonder List." Makes immediate sense.
3. Generally hyphenated.
4. Ha! Good voice here.
5. This makes him sound like a cast-off lamp. It raises questions. Did the family move recently? Did he go into a home? This detail sticks out and pulls me away from the narrative.
6. This paragraph is a list instead of a true description of plot. The specific events are glossed over ("series of mishaps"). The religious/big question element from the previous paragraph—not to mention the friendship with Naomi—is forgotten. I have a sense of the writer's themes, but not how they're organized into story, or who the key characters are.
7. Strong writing background here, and some diverse interests!
8. The writer can always give gatekeepers this option, but they will also want to make sure they present any material that's enclosed, e.g., "The first # of pages are pasted below." Also note if this is a simultaneous submission, no matter this writer's strong enthusiasm for this particular agent.

9. If the agent also represents this category, these are fine to mention, as long as the writer doesn't go into too much detail. My strong recommendation is to focus on one project per query.

MIDDLE GRADE QUERY #7 FEEDBACK

This query letter landed representation for the project, and that's great. There's strong voice here and a clear sense of story, which will focus on school, family, and the search for identity, which are perennial middle grade themes. I do have some recommendations here, however, for how it could've been stronger.

The second query meat paragraph is basically a list, and it doesn't come together into a linear plot. Consider this article:

"Query Letter Plot Pitch: Premise vs Plot"

There's also a bit of a disconnect between the initial meat paragraph and the next one. The first is all about the "Wonder List" and big life questions, as well as a relationship with Naomi. The second is all about some of Dani's other struggles at school and with her sister. The two don't feel cohesive right now, especially since the titular "Wonder List" never really comes back into the pitch.

Ideally, there would be a more chronological list of plot, key relationships would be clearly identified, and the "Wonder List" would make a repeat appearance to bring the query full circle.

As is, I have a sense of what the story is about in very broad terms, but I probably couldn't really imagine a specific scene or sequence of events from this novel with only this query to guide me. My preference would be for the writer to create more plot in the agent or publisher's head by clearly putting a few more events on the page.

MIDDLE GRADE QUERY #8 / FANTASY (402 WORDS)

DEAR AGENT,

Twelve[1]-year-old Takia and her cat, Pickle, need a magic[2] mentor. In a world where magic is woven from the bond between mage and animal, Takia can't wait to begin learning magic—as her two **nearly identical**[3] sisters already have. [Think of the power! The glory! Not to mention a whole new world of delicious mischief][4].

But just when Takia is clam-happy to have finally found a mentor, her younger brother disappears, [leaving only a slightly chewed and **oddly illustrated**[5] shoe to hint at what has happened to him][6]. Takia eagerly takes on the task of finding him. It's a puzzle and an adventure—two things she loves.

After deciphering the shoe's clue, Takia and Pickle learn that a corrupt police officer, Javard, has been kidnapping children, including her brother, and[7] forcing them to work in a secret factory where they're in danger of losing their ability to work[8] magic and perhaps worse[9]. [As the stakes turn serious][10], Takia must learn to weave not only magic, [but also more closely knit relationships with those around her][11]. Together, she and Pickle must find the factory and stop Javard before he destroys the futures of dozens of children[12].

Feline Magic is a completed **78,000-word**[13] upper middle grade fantasy. While it stands on its own as a novel, it is also the first of a planned trilogy ~~that follows a mounting movement for children's rights~~[14]. Feline Magic[15] will appeal to those who recently enjoyed the puzzles in Kevin Sands' *Blackthorn Key* series, the concern for animal rights in Linda Sue Park's *Wing & Claw* series, or the forefronting of children's voices in *Minnie McLary Speaks Her Mind,* [as well as those who, like me, grew up loving the magical mentorship in Tamora Pierce's *Circle of Magic* series, the human-daemon relationships in Philip Pullman's *His Dark Materials* series or the tea-infused friendships of E.L. Konigsburg's *The View From Saturday*][16].

When not writing fiction, I'm pursuing a PhD in philosophy at Georgetown University, specializing in ethics and law. I'm a member of SCBWI and founder of an active critique group. [Fiction provides me an alternate approach to the same sorts of issues I care about in my academic work][17]. [*Feline Magic,* for example, explores ethical and legal issues such as autonomy, empathy, implicit bias, animal ethics, child labor, and the dangers of police power][18].

[I hope you will consider representing it][19]. **The first XYZ pages are pasted below, per your submission guidelines. Please note that this is a simultaneous submission.** Thank you very much for your time.

Sincerely,

(Signature)

---

1. Generally, try to spell out ages and numbers under 10.
2. Try to avoid repeating distinctive words in close proximity. Rephrase this sentence to avoid *needing* the repetition.
3. "-ly" words don't take hyphenation. The writer will want to make sure they're avoiding grammar/mechanics errors in the query, since writing is their stock in trade.
4. Great voice here, and the fact that mischief is a priority tells me something about the character. Nicely done.
5. Another instance of an incorrectly hyphenated "-ly" suffix.
6. The very detailed description of the shoe pulls focus. In a query, every detail needs to be absolutely necessary.
7. This is a long sentence. Break it up for ease of reading.
8. Some more word echo here.

9. Don't merely hint at worse stakes. If they exist, specify them!
10. Same here. This *sounds* great, but the writer could be more specific.
11. Vague. Why is this important? Especially since the writer doesn't then mention a relationship with a person, the reader gets the impression that Takia teams up with her cat.
12. Does her magic have anything to do with it? The query starts with the idea of her magic. How might it come full circle?
13. For this phrasing, the writer should use a hyphen.
14. Get into the specifics later, if requested.
15. Keep the formatting consistent. If the writer has capitalized this elsewhere, they should do it here, too.
16. Great comps but too many. Pick three. Otherwise, there's simply too much going on. Make sure to prioritize the most recent comp titles possible.
17. This gets perhaps too cerebral and beside the point, especially for a query.
18. A lot of this is clear from the plot description, so I don't know if the writer needs to go out of their way and explain further.
19. Nice, but goes without saying. Omit.

MIDDLE GRADE QUERY #8 FEEDBACK

A STRONG PITCH in terms of both character and story. We get a sense of Takia and the situation that throws her into adventure. I would like for the writer to tie in the idea of magic, especially what makes *feline* magic special (other than the mage-animal bond). Middle grade fantasy is a big market. However, there is a lot of competition. Fantasy with magic abounds. Animal magic is also a common premise. So how is this particular worldbuilding going to stand out? Give agents and publishers something fun to imagine. Plus, returning to the idea of magic at the end of the query will bring the beginning full circle.

I'd avoid going into such thematic analysis as this writer does in the bio paragraph. The themes come across, so I don't know if we need to zero back in on them. Doing too much of this can seem ponderous, and this writer could stand to trim a few words from the letter, with a goal of getting to 350. Details like the "nearly identical sisters" and the emphasis on the shoe in the second query meat paragraph can also be tightened. Only include what's 100% necessary, focusing instead on the more relevant details of character, plot, and worldbuilding.

MIDDLE GRADE QUERY #9 (291 WORDS)

Dear Agent,

LUIGI FLIES THE COOP is a [buddy story with two principal characters][1], **a humorous middle-grade adventure novel complete at 35,765[2] words.**

Eleven-year-old~~,~~ Michael Bannigan [desperately wants to make the soccer team this year][3]. His single mom says it's not going to happen unless his math grades improve. And then there's George, his egomaniacal **rival** ~~competitor for a spot on the team~~, who will literally step on anyone in his way.

Luigi Falcone is a pasta-loving mob accountant who, [thanks to some Sicilian magic, is transformed into a parrot][4] just in time to escape the clutches of his boss, who wrongly thinks Luigi stole his money.

Luigi, who has no clue now to behave like a parrot, befriends Michael and convinces ~~him~~ **the boy** to **adopt him** ~~bring Luigi home~~. With a "no-pets" policy, Michael's mom is determined to find the bird's rightful owner. [It's a race against time as Luigi, with Michael's help, follows the clues to solve the mystery of the missing money before his boss's goons discover that Luigi-the-accountant is now Luigi-the-parrot][5].

In turn, Luigi helps Michael with his algebra homework and has his back when it comes to dealing with George. He even coaches Michael on how to make great pasta with marinara sauce[6]. [Ultimately, however, Michael must choose between competing in the final try-outs for a position on the team or coming to the rescue of his fine-feathered friend][7].

I am the author of *TRAVEL WITH OTHERS WITHOUT WISHING THEY'D STAYED HOME*, a Benjamin Franklin Silver Award winner, and two volumes of *SKIER'S GUIDE TO CALIFORNIA*[8]. I am also a member of the Author's Guild and SCBWI.

[Please let me know if you would like to read *LUIGI FLIES THE COOP*][9]. **Note that this is a simultaneous submission.** Thank you for your consideration.

Sincerely,

(Signature)

---

1. This term "buddy story" isn't technically a book category. The writer could use this intro paragraph to add more logistical information. I'm bringing content from a much later paragraph right up to the top.
2. The writer can round up. The exact number is too specific. This is also quite short for modern middle grade.
3. This sounds dire, but could use context. What, specifically and personally, does this mean to him, and why?
4. Whoa! Didn't see that coming. Is this an adult character? Who's now a parrot? Okay! I'm along for the ride. I just want to see how it all comes together.
5. To be honest, this sounds like Luigi's story. Making the soccer team pales in comparison to waking up as a parrot and having to escape a mob boss. The big problem with that? Luigi is an adult character. Michael, the kid, ends up playing second fiddle to him, and that's a big issue in a story pitched as middle grade.
6. But this has nothing to do with Michael's goals. This seems all about Luigi.
7. Michael's stakes (soccer vs. rescuing the parrot) are low compared to Luigi's stakes (stay a parrot vs. become a human, escape mob boss). This, again, doesn't make Michael's story seem nearly as compelling. Maybe giving Michael higher personal stakes for wanting to play soccer would help, but if his big plot point in the query is "algebra homework," I worry. Also, Luigi's conflict completely overtakes Michael's

and forces Michael into a choice that diminishes his experience and only benefits Luigi.

8. Do any of these have publishers and years that can be added?
9. Most agents and publishers want to see pages right off the bat. Instead of leaving this open-ended, send what the guidelines request. Gatekeepers will ask for *more* if they're interested, but it behooves every writer to send a writing sample right away, especially if the guidelines want one.

MIDDLE GRADE QUERY #9 FEEDBACK

FROM THE WRITER'S use of the term "buddy comedy," I wonder if they're steeped in the screenwriting/film world. I suspect this because one of the golden rules of screenwriting is to hit multiple demographics. Film studios want a role for kid actors in a family movie, sure, but they also need to give Tom Hanks something to do, because the adult role is going to be the star vehicle and moneymaker. Why am I rambling about film? Because this query for a middle grade novel makes it seem like the adult character (Luigi) has the more compelling story, and the kid character (Michael) is a throwaway.

Notice that Luigi is even the titular character, while Michael doesn't make the marquee. Even though Luigi is a parrot for most of the story (a more kid-friendly character than an accountant), he's still an adult in parrot form, with an adult mindset, adult experiences, and adult frames of reference for his life. The writer can't get around that, I don't think, by simply making him an animal.

Children's publishing has a lot of rules, some more arbitrary than others. But one of the most sacred is that children's books focus on child characters who are (approximately) the same age as the target audience. So a picture book wouldn't feature a twentysomething main character—it'd star a five-year-old. Young adult protagonists are usually sixteen or eighteen. And a middle grade novel would spotlight an eleven-year-old ... not a middle-aged accountant.

Yes, there is an eleven-year-old present, but he almost feels like a token because his concerns are the soccer team and the bully and homework (very standard for middle grade, so the writer will have to work even harder to make these elements seem fresh). Meanwhile, the adult character's concerns are a mob boss, and clearing his name, and *oh yeah*, HELP I'M A PARROT ALL OF A SUDDEN.

As a reader, I'd much rather experience the latter story than the former, but the protagonist question remains, as most middle grade novels don't spotlight adult perspectives. (And they especially don't provide an adult POV, though I'm not sure whether we'll be stepping into Luigi's lens here or merely seeing him through Michael's.)

If this was pitched as an adult project, no problem. But since this is being pitched as middle grade, there's a definite disconnect, and I just don't know if spinning the query to make Michael's story sound more high stakes will be *enough*. The issue of POV affects an entire manuscript, not just a pitch. An experienced middle grade agent or publisher is likely to come to the same conclusion and wonder whether the writer has chosen the right category.

MIDDLE GRADE QUERY #10 (366 WORDS)

Dear Agent,

August + Nora is a middle grade novel about an introvert and her robot. [While the story is about friendship, its sci-fi elements, world-building, and strong character development][1] will draw young readers in and, with any luck~~;~~, inspire a new generation of nerds[2]. The manuscript is complete at 26,000 words.

August is brilliant. At age ten, she's become a skillful mechanic. She spends all of her free time building, fixing, and programming robots. But that doesn't leave any time for socializing and August's mom is getting worried. [August goes through her school day ~~avoiding~~ **without** talking. When she gets home, it's up to her room. No adventures. No sleepovers. No friends][3].

When August fails to give out a single invitation for her **eleventh**[4] birthday party, it seems like she'll never make a friend. Until August gets an idea. Maybe she could literally *make*[5] a friend. She has the expertise and the spare parts—why not build a robot [and program it to be her friend?][6] August's idea seems even better after she finds a mysterious processor at Garbage Island. Mom has forbidden August from bringing processors home, because there's no telling what kind of programming they come with. But this processor has the power to handle some seriously complicated code and that's exactly what August needs.

After hours of research, coding, and building, August pushes the power button on her brand new, state-of-the-art friend. [And nothing goes according plan][7].

[Some comparable titles to *August + Nora* are:][8]

- *The Wild Robot* by Peter Brown (Little, Brown & Company, 2016)
- *The Miscalculations of Lightning Girl* by Stacy McAnulty (Random House, 2018)
- *The Science of Unbreakable Things* by Tae Keller (Random House, 2018)
- *Max Einstein: The Genius Experiment* by James Patterson (Little, Brown & Company, 2018)

[This is my first novel and it is the result of unending support from my wife and two kids, a crazy amount of Netflix binge watching, an even crazier amount of reading, and decades of daydreaming][9]. I have been an active member of SCBWI since 2014 and hold a Bachelor of Arts degree in English, Creative Writing from Michigan State University. **The first XYZ pages are enclosed, below.** This is a simultaneous submission. Thank you so much for your time!

Sincerely,

(Signature)

---

1. Good stuff, but break this sentence up, or readers will lose steam before they get to the joke at the end.
2. Ha! Good voice.
3. We're repackaging the same information here. The point is well-made. Do we need all of this?
4. Spell out ages.
5. I recommend italics here for emphasis. Though formatting can sometimes be scrambled in email, it's worth trying for the sake of voice.
6. This is already clear. Does it need further explanation?

7. I like the set-up for the cliffhanger here, but I'm looking for more meat about plot and character development. For this query, I'd recommend putting in more material from the second half. Agents and publishers will want to get a sense of the writer's plotting abilities beyond the first act.
8. The writer could condense this into a paragraph to avoid the long bullet list. I'd pick three strong comps, maximum.
9. Keep lists to three items maximum, as well. Otherwise, a sentence overloaded with elements tends to run long. Especially for the "personality" part of the bio. The writer might not want to put too much focus here, even if this is easy and breezy and fits the project's tone.

MIDDLE GRADE QUERY #10 FEEDBACK

THIS IS A REALLY fun and voice-driven query, which is great for middle grade. However, by putting a premium on voice, the writer tends to repeat information. Especially in the bit about August having no social life. They spin this data a few different ways because—it seems to me —they are pleased with their phrasing. And they're right to be satisfied, the voice is fun. But substance is more important than style in a query letter (don't get me wrong, the latter is nice, but it shouldn't overshadow a clear sense of story).

The choice to describe the set-up only (without getting into the rest of the plot) is also a potential shortcoming. Stopping here is a gamble, because this writer risks not giving gatekeepers enough information to make a decision. Sure, I'm curious about what happens on account of the cliffhanger, but not "request it just to scratch the itch" curious.

I'd rather be presented with more data about the writer's ability to plot. As is, the query covers (I'd imagine) 25% of the novel, right up to the point where August builds Nora, the other titular character, and that's it.

If I have to read an entire manuscript to find out what's being teased here, I'm not going to feel sufficiently compelled without more substance up front.

Some information is a lot more enticing to an agent or publisher than *no* information. Teasing works best when a writer deploys carefully chosen details, rather than totally withholding everything a reader might want to know.

MIDDLE GRADE QUERY #11 / FANTASY (304 WORDS)

Dear Agent,

Because of your success with (Comp Titles), I hope that you will be interested in THE ONE-CHANCE SPELL, a 51,000-word MG fantasy adventure [for fans of William Alexander, Jonathan Auxier, and Karen Foxlee][1].

Twelve-year-old Sally Penrod doesn't know anything about her family[2]—save that someone bequeathed her a blank book with the cryptic message: *May she have many chances.* [She doesn't know why she's the only one in her school who can read the ancient texts abandoned in the basement. And she certainly doesn't know why people think she can find the lost book of the Logomotor King, who Splintered the world and set goblins against humans][3]. All she knows is that despite her "gift for words," she's just as lonely as ever.

Then Sally meets Rumble, and it doesn't matter that [he's better dressed and citrus-obsessed][4]. What matters is that he loves books, thinks smart, and considers Sally his "truest, bestest" friend. [What matters to everyone else, though, is that Rumble's a goblin][5].

[Soon, the two friends must combine their wits to survive drunken mobs, political intrigue, and four-hour scrivener exams][6]. When Sally's blank book turns out to contain the world's most powerful spells[7], she suddenly finds herself an unlikely heroine: only she can stop the looming war between humans and goblins. Little does she realize[8] that her "gift for words" may be the very weapon that endangers her friend and Splinters the world for good.

Recent recognition for my fiction includes: 2016 *Fairy Tale Review* prose finalist, 2017 WNDB middle-grade mentorship winner, and 2017 Katherine Paterson Prize middle-grade-category winner. My picture book, LEAF MAN, with husband-illustrator Chris O'Leary, will be published in 2019 by Albert Whitman[9].

I've included the first chapter (about ten pages) below and would be thrilled to hear from you. **Please note that this is a simultaneous submission.** Many thanks for your time and consideration!

Best regards,

(Signature)

---

1. This is a great logistical opening paragraph containing the personalization, manuscript statistics, and nice comps.
2. Maybe "her real family" or "her birth family" here to be more specific? Unless she's currently living with no family at all, which may be hard to believe for this age.
3. The writer is presenting the information in the negative. Instead of phrasing this as all the stuff she *doesn't* know, focus on the information itself. "All she knows is that she can read the texts ... And people seem convinced that she can find ... She just doesn't know why." This approach focuses on what is actually happening, rather than her confusion about it.
4. These details seem rather arbitrary, with a goofy unintentional (?) rhyme.
5. Good. Maybe add some stakes to the social climate, which we already know is anti-goblin. What are the specific ramifications of a human/goblin friendship?
6. A list that doesn't give me a sense of narrative flow, the importance of these events, or their proper order. This doesn't actually convey structure.
7. The writer will want to be clear about the magical worldbuilding. What kind of magic can Sally do? What's the magic foundation of the world?
8. The writer's focus has been heavy on stuff Sally doesn't know. This makes her sound like a pretty impotent protagonist. I'd avoid this. I really like the high stakes here, but I'd try to get away from describing her as quite so hapless.

9. Great bio! If a writer has many writing credits, they should focus on the biggest, most noteworthy, and most recent. This writer has a lot to their name, but this is a nice length for a bio paragraph, which means they've been selective.

MIDDLE GRADE QUERY #11 FEEDBACK

This is a compelling query for a fantasy. There are just a few holes to fill. Initially, Sally doesn't know much and it's relatable and charming, but it quickly makes me worry about whether or not she's competent enough to drive a story.

After all, a character who wanders around "dunno-ing" isn't going to be compelling (and a lot of manuscripts suffer from this issue, so agents and publishers will be wary). The list in the middle of the query meat could be fleshed out, too. Consider this article:

"Query Letter Plot Pitch: Premise vs Plot"

Finally, there's a lot of focus on the mysterious notebook, which does come back into play. But the "May she have many chances" message, while cryptic and enticing, is not given any more attention. I'd love for it to come full circle for the purpose of the query. The writer could also do more to establish the specific stakes for the goblin rift and the kind of magic that Sally ends up doing with the help of her book.

Goblin fantasy novels exist in the marketplace. As do magic fantasy novels. To be competitive, the writer should emphasize the book's unique worldbuilding, magic, or stakes. How is *this* goblin novel going to be different? How is *this* magic going to stand out? Use the query to subtly pitch this book's unique selling proposition by defining these a bit more.

MIDDLE GRADE QUERY #12 (220 WORDS)

Agent[1]

Literary Agency

Dear Agent,

[Congratulations on helping to bring outstanding books to kids for over two decades][2]. I'm pleased to present my contemporary middle grade novel, *Title,* for your consideration.

[In this comedy of confusion][3], twelve-year-old Emma has everything she needs to succeed in show **business ... [except**[4] permission from her mother][5]. In addition[6], a family secret and a friend's betrayal also [threaten her path to fame][7].

When Emma finally wins a role in a major motion picture, she's beyond **happy ... for** about three minutes. Now she must figure out how to keep it a secret from her parents. Emma maneuvers over this hurdle with a small white lie[8] only to discover she's being spied upon. Problems escalate until Emma is accused of leaking plot secrets and dismissed from the movie[9]. Emma must find her betrayer and win her role back before the director finds[10] a new star to take her place. In the end, Emma is forced to choose between ~~her own~~ success [and a promise she made to a friend][11].

Title is my 42,000-word debut novel[12]. I have ~~an~~ English and French Literature degree**s** from Stanford University, and I'm an active member of SCBWI and an online critique group.

I have pasted a synopsis and sample pages below, as requested[13]. **Please note that this is a simultaneous submission.** Thank you for your time. I look forward to hearing from you.

Sincerely,

(Signature)

---

1. This type of heading is a letter writing convention, less often used in email. Skip it.
2. This rings a bit like flattery. I'd probably try a softer approach or something more personal. Is there a specific client or title from the agent's list that makes sense to mention here?
3. Sounds good, but without context, it doesn't mean much to an outside reader. I don't actually know if "confusion" is a selling point. Maybe more of a "comedy of errors" description, which is a familiar term in literature.
4. Use spaces before and after an ellipsis in an ongoing sentence.
5. The voice is a bit formal here. Try something like "Mom's permission" to instantly make it more colloquial.
6. Some redundancy here, which is indicated with underlines.
7. Presenting these events in more detail will help the plot seems specific. As part of the logline, these seem tacked-on. If the writer wants to use a one-sentence pitch, they could focus on the first sentence of this paragraph.
8. The phrase "little white lie" is so common that I wonder why it's not used here.
9. The writer could go a bit deeper. Who are the suspects, and why might someone be betraying Emma? Maybe present the reader with more context.
10. Word echo (repetition of words or phrases in close proximity).
11. I worry this is too vague. Especially since the pitch deals so much with betrayal. If Emma is being betrayed, maybe by a friend, why would this promise be so important? If you're going to use this as the last line of the query meat, I'd go into a bit more detail.
12. I'm afraid that terms like "debut novel" or "pre-published" (for a project that hasn't sold yet) come across as a bit presumptuous. I'm not sure they set the right tone, even if they are validating to use and are meant to convey confidence.
13. There's a difference between an agent's request and a cold submission. This makes it sound like it was personally requested. If it wasn't, the writer should avoid this implication with "per your guidelines," or similar, instead.

MIDDLE GRADE QUERY #12 FEEDBACK

In this query, the logline could stand alone with just the first sentence, rather than adding the second sentence, which feels a bit more vague. Consider this article:

"Query Letter Plot Pitch: Premise vs Plot"

There are also some moments of "pitchy" language, which sounds good, but doesn't actually provide any context or detail. Consider this article:

"Concrete Writing: Using Specific Language"

I'd really zero in on the betrayal part of the plot, because Emma's relationships seem to be important to the story but aren't explored that much. Especially since a potentially bad relationship is threatening her shot at stardom, give this part of the character's life more attention.

The stakes of potentially losing her dream are really well-established here, so I'd like to understand the threat to her movie role more clearly as a key to understanding the story. Here, it seems the writer wants to create intrigue, but this makes the central conflict seem hazy.

Everyone reading this book should remember to let the important elements stand out clearly in the query. Don't play tricks or be cute about the crucial scaffolding of your novel.

On the sentence level, I'd encourage this writer to avoid the word echo of "find" and "finds" and to reconsider using "In addition" and "also," because they serve the same function in the sentence.

Otherwise, this is a strong query. A few tone adjustments (the congratulations note at the beginning and the "debut novel" phrasing near the end) would make it even more compelling.

MIDDLE GRADE QUERY #13 / FANTASY (368 WORDS)

(DATE)

Agent Name

Agency Name[1]

Dear Agent:

[I'm querying you because…] I'm hoping you'll enjoy *Not Your Typical Troll*, a contemporary middle grade fantasy complete at 58,000 words. [It explores family and friendships, living up to expectations, and the sometimes blurry line between right and wrong from a humorous first-person perspective][2].

Magic is the one thing seventh grader Slam Stranglehold is good at. [Troll's truth, he's not stubborn, or brave, or destined for a career as a professional wrestler, like his parents hope][3]. But his magic experiments must be kept secret, safe between the pages of his notebook, [because using all but the bare minimum necessary to disguise his troll appearance from humans has been forbidden since a treaty was made between humans and Mythicals hundreds of years ago][4].

So when Slam is caught using magic by his witchy teacher (in both senses of the word)[5], he tries a spell that inadvertently diverts the blame from **him—and** onto his dwarf friend Mica. When Slam realizes that the Council of Mythicals is punishing Mica for his crime, he sets out to make things right, [and finds himself in an unlikely alliance with Mica's friend Clover to find and free Mica][6]. To his surprise, he discovers he wasn't the only one using magic: there's a secret Movement to restore the right to use magic to every Mythical. [And the Council—and its self-serving, magic-wielding members—will do anything to stop the Movement: even force Slam to identify who's behind it][7]. [Under threat of failing his Troll Trials and becoming the biggest loser in troll history, Slam must make some tough choices: make his family proud by ignoring Mica's plight—and the lure of magic—to cooperate with the Council … or aid the Movement and free Mica while exposing his own biggest secret][8].

Most trolls wouldn't lose any sleep over the plight of a dwarf, the imminent showdown between the Council and the Movement, or his secret fear that he's not "troll enough" to pass his Troll Trials, but Slam's not your typical troll. [And the Trials just might force him to prove it][9].

I am a member of the SCBWI, and write both middle-grade and picture books.

Per your guidelines, the first XYZ pages are pasted below. Please note that this is a simultaneous submission. Thank you! I look forward to hearing from you.

Sincerely,

(Signature)

---

1. There's no pressure to use these letter writing conventions in an email query. I'd omit this.
2. Good statement about theme, and nice manuscript logistics. I know exactly what I'm getting into here, and the story seems like it will dovetail really well with the middle grade market. This writer comes off as savvy!

3. Great. This really plunges us into the voice and world with "Troll's truth" and the idea that the pinnacle of achievement for a troll is a professional wrestling career. Ha!
4. Whoa whoa whoa. This sentence offers a lot of good stuff, but it is also quite long. The writer introduces many worldbuilding ideas here. The character is hiding his troll identity, he does it with magic, that's forbidden, etc. Break this up and take some time to get it right. Does he live in the human world or the troll world? What if his troll identity is discovered? Start there and build stakes. *Then* go into the other things his magic can do, since it seems that he has to keep his talents hidden. Otherwise, there's good tension in this idea of living a double life.
5. Ha!
6. Necessary? This is a lot of detail and introduces a character who doesn't come back into the pitch. I'd omit.
7. Queries are meant to be read quickly. This is a lot of information for one sentence. Try to break it up.
8. Another blockbuster sentence. I love the high stakes here but, boy, are they tough to keep straight with all of this detail coming at once.
9. I'm a little lost here on one thing: Slam possesses, apparently, above-average magic. But then why is he at risk for not passing the Troll Trials? Why isn't he "troll enough"? He is pitched as an above-average troll, if anything. This pulls me out of the query a bit.

MIDDLE GRADE QUERY #13 FEEDBACK

THERE ARE great stakes in this query. And the writer plunges the reader right into the troll world. This has the hallmarks of a compelling fantasy, with political unrest, restrictions on magic, and a character having to make some hard moral choices (doing the right thing by others vs. protecting himself and getting ahead). But I get a little confused toward the end about the Troll Trials, and why Slam's above-average magic would somehow result in him being not "troll enough." This logic merits a second look.

Finally, I'd urge the writer to look at some of their long, complex sentences. Queries are meant to be read quickly, and with all the em-dashes, ellipses, and additional clauses tacked on after colons ... it doesn't make for easy reading. All of the information is good, but the aim here is to present it as clearly as possible. I'd recommend that the writer read the entire query aloud and mark where they might be running out of breath. They should take some of the pressure off of each individual sentence do it all, all at once.

MIDDLE GRADE QUERY #14 (260 WORDS)

Dear Agent,

We met at the______ [writing conference in October, where I sat at the same lunch table as you][1]. At that time, you said you'd accept my submission of my middle grade novel ~~for consideration~~, *Finding My Way Home* ~~is a middle grade novel~~, **which is** complete at 35,000 words~~,~~ ~~that~~ **and** explores the loving, yet frustrating relationship between eleven-year-old Jodi and her six-year-old autistic brother**,** Tyler.

Jodi has the support of her three friends, "The Butterfly Bunch," to help her cope, but[2] loses them when her mother decides the family must move to New Jersey so Tyler can attend a better school. ***What about me?***[3] Jodi wonders. *Is everything about Tyler?*[4] When the class bully targets Jodi at her new school, she longs to return to Ohio. When[5] she's trapped with him in an elevator on a field trip to the Museum of Natural History, Jodi realizes he's acting out his frustration because he also has a brother with a disability. [New friends can be found under the strangest circumstances][6].

Like Jodi, thousands of siblings have a brother or sister with special needs. Few middle grade novels, like Cynthia Lord's *Rules*, speak to their issues. [And every child, handicapped sibling or not, feels that the other child gets more attention][7].

I am a psychologist and parent of two children, one with autism. My work has appeared in *Highlights, Goldfinch,* and *Write Now* literary magazines and I've edited and written for newsletters. I'm a member of SCBWI.

You can find the first XYZ pages pasted below. Please note that this is a simultaneous submission. Thank you for your time, and I hope you'll want to read more of *Finding My Way Home*.

(Signature)

---

1. A good detail about a previous meeting, which the writer should definitely mention. But is there any *other* reason they want to submit to this person? The fact that they've shared oxygen in the same room is not necessarily personally compelling. Agents want to think that there are other reasons (their work, for example) for writers to submit to them, other than the fact that they're a warm body with a slush pile.
2. Break into a new sentence, as the stakes are raised here.
3. Verbatim thoughts are usually formatted in italics. Consider this article: "Formatting Interiority"
4. Good. Her pain is evident here without the writer telling the reader.
5. Avoid starting two sentences in a row with the same phrasing.
6. A good theme, but this is a bit vague. Is the elevator the strange circumstance? The friendship with an apparent bully? The writer should also weave these events back into the established plot.
7. A bit unclear. Every child with a handicapped sibling? But when the writer then says "handicapped sibling or not," and I get confused. Do they mean "every child" in the world? What about only children? They don't have an "other child" in their lives. I get what the writer is trying to say, but the phrasing could be more precise. Broad generalizations, even if extremely well-intentioned, tend to diminish the credibility of a writer's claims.

MIDDLE GRADE QUERY #14 FEEDBACK

A STRONG QUERY insofar as Jodi's experience goes. Her conflict is clear. She wants to have her own life and feels like she's in her brother's shadow, especially when Mom makes decisions that are best for him but happen to disregard her. Then there's the plot element of the bully and a moment of unexpected understanding. Good.

The writer starts on a very strong note of family conflict. Then we get school conflict. These are usually the two main elements of contemporary middle grade (unless the project is fantasy or sci-fi).

After this, though, the writer shifts gears. The query doesn't go back to the family side of things. Jodi has a surprising encounter in an elevator. And a realization. And? So? The query also doesn't "zoom out" to show how Jodi applies what she's realized. The pitch feels incomplete. The writer should bring it back full circle to the wider implications for Jodi's family life.

There's a strong bio here, with good and extremely relevant life, professional, and writing credentials. The market is looking for more stories of diverse lived experiences, so the autism plot is timely, and the writer's personal history with it gives me the sense that it will be deeply and sensitively handled.

MIDDLE GRADE QUERY #15 / CONTEMPORARY (342 WORDS)

Received Representation!

Dear Agent,

[From your manuscript wishlist, I see you love big oafish dogs. My middle grade caper features a Giant Schnauzer named Benz who plays a key role—he even dresses in an Elvis costume for a pet parade][1]. With that in mind, I'm pleased to offer FAUX REAL, which is complete at 42,000 words.

Twelve-year-old Tru Diaz craves acceptance from her classmates, even if it means ~~chasing fashion trends and~~ wearing pleather cowboy boots in 120-degree Las Vegas heat. Her parents ask her to help at their family-owned pawn shop while they perform as Elvis and Marilyn Monroe **impersonators**. While Tru's watching the store, the cutest boy in school shows up. To impress him, [she takes out an invaluable item —Elvis's mortuary toe tag—and doesn't notice when someone steals it off the counter][2]. The owner, who looks and talks like a mobster, is coming to redeem it in six days and[3] if she can't find the heirloom, [Tru's family will lose everything][4].

Tru creates a fake toe tag, then starts chasing down suspects. In the process, she crashes a casino and accuses her crush **of the theft**. Tru tracks **a lead**[5] to the The King of Rock 'N' Roll World Convention. [The only problem is, ever since a gang of Elvi robbed the pawn shop the year before, she panics when there's more than one in the same room][6]. As she faces her fears, Tru is shocked to learn who stole the toe tag and why. [However, to do the right thing means she might be forever banished to the loser lunchroom table][7].

FAUX REAL is ***Ocean's Eleven***[8]—at ElvisCon. [It explores how in a world filled with fakes, not being true to yourself is the greatest deception of all][9].

My experience as a journalist includes publishing more than 350 articles in national and regional magazines, and [five novelty science books for children][10]. I'm a member of SCBWI, and oversee communications and edit **the** *KiteTales* newsletter for our local chapter.

Thank you for your time and consideration. **Please find the first XYZ pages pasted below. Note that this is a simultaneous submission.** I look forward to hearing from you.

Sincerely,

(Signature)

---

1. Ha! Not every bit of personalization needs to be serious. This will be a refreshing change of pace in the slush.
2. Good. In this story world, it is a *big* deal, I'd imagine, that Dad plays Elvis for a living. The stakes in humorous stories tend to be less serious, but they still need to seem like they matter to the character.
3. Break up this sentence. Queries are meant to be read quickly, and humorous voice works best when it's short and punchy.
4. I believe it because the client is a mobster. Great stakes!
5. This is a cosmetic change because I suggested the writer add "theft" to the previous sentence, so they wouldn't want to use "thief" in the next sentence.
6. Ha! A *ridiculous* complication, but it makes sense in this humorous story world.
7. Hmm. This falls flat for two reasons. She already seems like a misfit, no matter how hard she tries, so this might already be her reality. Second, it gets extremely vague. If there's a good twist, I'm of the school that the query should reveal it so that agents and publishers can see the writer's plotting chops at work.

8. If you're citing a title, movie, or publication, make sure the spelling and formatting are accurate.
9. I love this as a logline, but it's wordy. Try to rephrase.
10. Care to cite a publisher?

MIDDLE GRADE QUERY #15 FEEDBACK

WHAT I LOVE about this example is that it proves that funny, quirky stories *can* and *should* also have plot and stakes. Even the ridiculous can seem serious and compelling under the right circumstances. What this writer does really well is create urgency by defining *why* the plot matters. A mobster coming to get something from the family pawn shop is a very real threat, even if the item is totally off-the-wall. This proves that it's less about *what* a writer puts into a query, and more about creating a sense of *why it matters to the character*. The latter is what will sell the reader on a particular story. It's also how a writer gets a reader to care. This is a very important lesson that could be applied to many queries in this guide.

Young Adult Queries

YOUNG ADULT QUERY #1 (230 WORDS)

DEAR AGENT,

Valencia Roberts, [Shaved Ice Hut employee and aspiring gastroenterologist][1], can't wait for the all-night company retreat at Seven Seas Water Park. Not only will she be able to spend time with her co-worker/girl-crush Carmen, [but she'll also get the chance to prove to management that she's supervisor material][2].

The only downside: her nemesis, the lifeguard Bryce Dawson, will also be there. Which might give Val the perfect opportunity to exact revenge for what he did to her sister the previous summer ... [as long as she can avoid getting caught by his dad, who happens to be the general manager][3].

But when her register comes up $100 short, Val is suddenly in danger of losing the job she depends on[4]. Convinced that Bryce is trying to sabotage her, Val becomes determined to prove he took the money. During a team-building treasure hunt that soon spirals out of control, Val's plan unravels when [she discovers that Seven Seas is in danger of closing for good—unless she and her co-workers can figure out how to save it][5].

CAPTAIN VALENCIA, a YA mystery[6] complete at 50,000 words, was inspired by the summers I spent working at a water park. I have since moved on from shaving ice for a living; my professional background is in nutritional science, and my research has been published in peer-reviewed journals.

The first XYZ pages are pasted below, per your guidelines. Please note that this is a simultaneous submission. Thank you for your time and consideration.

Sincerely,

(Signature)

---

1. Ha! Great intro with a little bit of humor here to set the tone of the query and project.
2. Raise the stakes. Why is this important to Val? Sure, promotions are obviously desirable, but I want the personal stakes for this particular character.
3. A roundabout way of introducing the big conflict, and vague. What happened? Why is it important to exact revenge? Is this her sister's battle to fight, or hers? This makes me wonder even more about *her* story.
4. This seems like the big conflict, at last. Specifics help readers understand the character's situation and what makes her tick, what her value system is, etc. Emphasize why this matters.
5. Again, this doesn't seem like her battle, exactly. These things (the prank against her sister, the park closing) are happening to others. I want to see Val at the center of her own story, so consider making it more personal to her. (This could also be a story issue, rather than a query issue.)
6. I'm not entirely sure I'm seeing the mystery angle as much. It seems Bryce is a likely candidate for the theft, unless there's going to be a subverted expectation here. Does this refer to the secret that the water park is closing? Or the secret of *why* it's closing? (The latter doesn't seem as personally connected to Val and her story, as this would be a much bigger event for the actual owners.)

YOUNG ADULT QUERY #1 FEEDBACK

THIS QUERY DOES a good job of presenting plot, but isn't as successful at handling character and stakes. As I mention in the footnotes, there's a lot of focus on events that happen in the larger story world (some drama with the sister and the water park) but not necessarily how these tie back to the protagonist. The closest we get is learning that Val "depends on" her job, but why? Is her family in dire straits? Does she need this job because it informs her identity, or is it just a means to an end?

A lot might be implied, but I'd prefer that it be more explicit so the reader gets a stronger sense of this protagonist and the conflict in her own story. That's really the concern here. Is she a proactive character, or is all of this tangentially related stuff simply happening *to* her in this plot? Obviously, for a compelling novel, the former is going to be more desirable.

Consider this article:

"Writing a Proactive Protagonist"

YOUNG ADULT QUERY #2 (293 WORDS)

Dear Agent,

[Seventeen-year-old Virginia makes bad choices. In fact, she's That Kind of Girl, according to the whispers][1]. The gossip (true or false) doesn't bother Virginia. As long as she has her ride-or-die group of girlfriends. Until she spends some quality time with Rumi, Safia's boyfriend. [Breaking with tradition, she doesn't sleep with Rumi. Worse, she falls in love with him][2].

Things get (even more) complicated when she discovers that somebody from her past has targeted Rumi's little sister and only Virginia knows[3]. He continues to be a respected member of the community and a friend of her parents. [Virginia knows she has to come forward][4].

Virginia can only protect Rumi's sister [with the support of her friends][5]. But her feelings for off-limits-Rumi continue to grow. [It's only a matter of time before somebody finds out][6].

[Just as Virginia realizes how much she needs her badass and beautiful girl group, she's also on the verge of destroying it][7].

EVER SINCE is contemporary YA and is complete at 70,000 words. It will (hopefully)[8] appeal to fans of Nina LaCour and Akemi Bowman[9].

I am a Seattle native, but for no good reason moved to Lincoln, Nebraska a couple of years ago. Now I do daily battle with three minions of Satan (my children), and in my off time (wait, I have no off time) stare at a wall and wonder why I have three kids. [In the middle of the night when I should be sleeping, I worry about commas, and alternately weep at the futility of it all, and yell into the void about what a genius I am][10].

Per your submission guidelines, the first XYZ pages are pasted below. Please note that this is a simultaneous submission. Thank you for your time and consideration,

(Signature)

---

1. A grabby, voice-driven opening to the query. I'd maybe recommend that the writer join this with the following paragraph. There's no need for a big break here.
2. Great voice. I like the idea that there's something worse than simply sleeping with a friend's boyfriend. I do worry about the infidelity aspect, per the following feedback chapter.
3. Unclear. Only Virginia knows that the sister is targeted? Or only Virginia knows who the offender is? Also, "targeted" is vague. For bullying? Sexual assault? Be clear here. This is the first big plot point that's described after Virginia connects with Rumi, so it needs to stand out.
4. A good opportunity to ramp up stakes. And? So? What if she does? What if she doesn't?
5. Unclear if Safia knows about the Rumi thing yet. Maybe the writer should specify, as each would have different ramifications.
6. Ah, good. Maybe make it clear earlier that this love develops in secret to raise the stakes throughout. Now that I think about it, I don't yet know whether Rumi is part of this infatuation and is reciprocating. Or is Virginia more in love with him than he is with her? That might be another piece of data to add. Is he clueless or very casual about it? Or is he falling for her, too? Each of these options would change the pitch.
7. Restating the idea of "with the support of her friends." Maybe save that for this paragraph?
8. Omit. Be confident!
9. Good comps!
10. Voice in a query is great. This may be too much voice/personality, though. The bio pulls focus, but it shouldn't.

YOUNG ADULT QUERY #2 FEEDBACK

THE WRITER DOES a great job of presenting a tough situation. A girl is torn between her friends and a forbidden love. Meanwhile, there's a potentially dangerous conflict unfolding. Ideally, the "someone from her past"/Remi's sister thing would be presented in a more specific way to raise stakes. Also, I suggest making it clear that the love is secret sooner. The writer should also clarify whether Rumi reciprocates Virginia's feelings. (Also, why doesn't *he* help his own sister?)

The query starts on this tense note of Virginia and her reputation, rumors, etc. But that completely falls away. I'm also not sure that all agents and acquiring editors will be able to overlook the idea that this protagonist is cheating (either emotionally or physically) with her best friend's boyfriend.

It might seem moralistic to some, but I have personally seen books with a cheating plot strike out on submissions to publishers, with infidelity explicitly cited as a dealbreaker for teen audiences. Cheating happens in adult-targeted fiction, but in YA, it seems like a touchy issue. It's also one of those "you made your bed, now sleep in it" flavors of self-inflicted suffering, which tends to make the character's conflict less sympathetic.

Speaking of sympathetic, Victoria claims to love her girl group, but is also "on the verge of destroying it," which doesn't exactly track. These ideas seem mutually exclusive, but that dissonance isn't really covered in the query, nor is Victoria described as having a redemption arc. It's suggested that she's heroic in the sister conflict, but I'm guessing here.

The writer starts on this reputation angle but doesn't do anything with it by the end of the query, which is not entirely satisfying and doesn't resolve the question of whether this protagonist's behavior is redeeming. There's also the coy suggestion that her bad rap might not valid "(true or not)." But given everything we learn, the bad reputation seems earned. Ideally, the query pitch will come full circle, with a nod to the beginning near the end. This doesn't happen here.

Finally, the writer might want to avoid having quite *so* much personality in the bio paragraph. Right now, it's pulling focus from the story. Tone down the jokes and voice, even if they're appealing (I bet this section was fun to write). Right now, the tone of this part of the query doesn't match the more serious-sounding plot.

YOUNG ADULT QUERY #3 / MULTIPLE POV (384 WORDS)

DEAR AGENT,

[I am writing to query you][1] for my dual-POV YA contemporary fantasy novel, MEMENTO MORI. (Personalization here.)

As the daughter of "America's First Gay Reality TV Ghost Hunters," Logan Ortiz-Woodley is accustomed to a life of LA luxury and semi-fame. [But when her fathers' show is defunded, Logan is forced to move to Snakebite, the rural Oregon town where her fathers grew up][2]. And Snakebite is everything she expects—big trucks, country music, and rampant homophobia. [But something deeper and darker is at work in Snakebite, too][3]. [After the disappearance of the town's golden-boy quarterback][4], Logan's fathers become the prime suspects in a murder investigation that shatters Snakebite's peaceful facade[5].

Enter Ashley Barton, girlfriend of the missing boy and daughter of Snakebite's self-appointed mayor. Like everyone else in town, Ashley suspects the Ortiz-Woodleys ~~are involved in her boyfriend's disappearance~~—[until she sees Tristan's ghost][6] [and the dark corners of Snakebite that she feared as a child return][7]. [With Ashley's knowledge of Snakebite and Logan's knowledge of the paranormal, the girls work

~~must~~ together as reluctant allies to solve Tristan's disappearance and stop the killer that stalks Snakebite][8].

While her fathers work to clear their name, [Logan digs into the dark history of Snakebite[9] and discovers she may know less about her family than she thought][10]. As Ashley fights her way closer to Tristan, her every step is haunted by Snakebite's [traditions of hate and exclusion][11]. [As the death toll rises, Ashley and Logan realize that their only chance of survival is each other][12].

MEMENTO MORI [is a story of legacies of hate, painful family dynamics, and the way true connection can fight back impending darkness][13]. It combines the atmosphere of V.E. Schwab's CITY OF GHOSTS with the tangled small-town dynamics of the CW's Riverdale. As a queer woman, I am excited to combine[14] queer characters with speculative fiction in a way I desperately wanted when I was a teen reader. I graduated from Pacific Lutheran University in 2016 with a degree in Creative Writing and Publishing.

MEMENTO MORI is complete at 92,000 words. Per submission guidelines, I have pasted the first (x **pages]** below. **Please note that this is a simultaneous submission.**

Thank you, and I look forward to hearing from you!

(Signature)

---

1. Stating the obvious. "I'm querying you with TITLE because ..." is more specific.
2. Great. The writer dives right into the inciting incident here.
3. This sentence raises the stakes. Good instinct.
4. Is this just a random murder victim? Or does he have any connection to Logan or her family?
5. Does this ring true if the town is described elsewhere as overtaken by "rampant homophobia"? From everything said about Snakebite so far, I'm not sure I'm getting even the illusion of "peaceful" anywhere.
6. If there's an actual paranormal element, I'd work that into the story earlier. The writer does say "fantasy," but ghosts are typically filed under "paranormal." Most readers know that reality TV is fake. TV ghost hunters have little to do with actual ghosts, so make it clear whether ghosts are, indeed, real in this world. Also, who is the "she" here? The grammar points to Ashley, but I feel like this was intended to refer to Logan instead.

7. I recommend introducing specifics about this sooner, instead of springing this information seemingly out of the blue.
8. I'd join this with the below paragraph, actually. Let Logan have her paragraph, let Ashley have hers, and then the story comes together. This is a smart way to approach a multiple POV query.
9. Why does Logan need Ashley for "local knowledge" if her dads are from Snakebite originally?
10. This is the second reference to the town's dark history, but it doesn't offer any more substance that the first reference.
11. The writer keeps talking about the darkness in Snakebite, the darkness of the past, etc. I wonder whether this is too nebulous right now.
12. One thing I'd like clarified: What, if anything, do ghosts have to do with the killer? Right now, that and "the darkness in Snakebite" seem sort of related, but these threads are not lighting up for me as entirely cohesive.
13. More vagueness. This sounds good but doesn't tell me much. I'd avoid thematic analysis here.
14. Avoid repeating words in close proximity.

YOUNG ADULT QUERY #3 FEEDBACK

THIS SOUNDS twisty and dark and promising for the YA market, which loves a murder thriller. The LGBTQIA+ element (told by a writer who lives that experience) is appealing in today's publishing landscape as well. The dual narrative POV is presented nicely. However, certain elements of the pitch suffer from vagueness. Consider this article:

"Concrete Writing: Using Specific Language"

We know there's homophobia, a "dark" town, a killer, and a ghost, but how do they all combine? The girls are in conflict, but thrown together rather haphazardly. The reason for this feels flimsy. What else connects them, other than the writer wanting to include an "odd couple" frenemy relationship in the plot?

The reader is going to be brand new to the story. The writer will want to pull these disparate strands together so the light bulb goes off and the reader gets a sense of the novel's full scope. I'd prefer the writer spend their word count doing this, rather than explaining their themes, which are explored in perhaps too much detail in the bio paragraph.

YOUNG ADULT QUERY #4 (304 WORDS)

(Date)[1]

Dear Agent:

Allow me to introduce Colby Kendricks: 80s music addict, high school basketball team wash out, and girlfriend-deficient dude who's trapped in a no-man's [land ~~that is neither~~ **between** nerd **and** jock][2]. At least he has a killer soundtrack queued up for what he's sure is going to be his comeback summer[3], [just as soon as he gets with the most sought-after cheerleader in his Colorado mountain town][4].

But when Colby makes a stupid and expensive mistake**,** he has to serve hard time at a summer job that stinks—literally**. I**t's the local PetsMall—and he doesn't even like animals. It's bad enough his childhood nemesis is sporting an assistant manager badge and wants revenge ~~for past grudges~~, but[5] he's also saddled with a PETA-approved, tree-hugging coworker from California he could so easily hate if she wasn't kind of hot. [When he finds himself sucked into a complicated relationship with both California Girl and a lovable rescue dog with a looming date on death row—just as his chance with the cheerleader finally opens up—he has to decide, in the immortal words of The Fixx][6]: will he stand, or will he fall?

[Funny, poignant, and brimming with insights into the (in)human condition][7], PET SHOP BOY: A SUMMER SOUNDTRACK (YA Contemporary/50,000 words) is the story of a mostly ordinary dude with extraordinary taste in music [who learns that the road to redemption is often found in forgiving the worst in a person … even if that person is yourself][8].

While my first love is writing YA fiction, by day I'm an online university writing instructor for international students. I also volunteer as a leader for a youth group of teen girls, [who humor me by serving as my insightful beta readers][9].

I've included the first chapter of my manuscript below. **Please note that this is a simultaneous submission.** [Would you like to read more?][10]

All best,

(Signature)

---

1. Most queries will be done via email. This is an old chestnut left over from written letter formatting. Omit.
2. The change I'm suggesting would make the phrasing less wordy. YA is all about voice, so it's important that the query flows. Speaking of which, this list of attributes, while fun, is a bit long. Queries are meant to be read quickly. It's also not as helpful to describe the character's situation and leave it at that. Focus on sequential plot and emphasize cause and effect.
3. This also begs the question of why he's a "wash out" and what he's coming back from. The writer could plant some tension/stakes here.
4. Ha! If humor works for the voice, it's always good to include it in the query (to a point, otherwise it gets gimmicky).
5. Break into two sentences.
6. Good stuff but crammed into one sentence. The query really skims over something that seems important (the rescue dog) by lumping this all together. See the feedback chapter that follows.
7. This is cute, but it also sounds like the writer is tooting their own horn with "funny" and "poignant." I'd rather the writer reserve judgment of their own work, especially glowing praise.
8. There is zero focus on what Colby needs to redeem himself for here, which is a big missed opportunity. I have no sense of who he is, what he's running from, what he wants to change, or what the stakes are if he doesn't grow. What makes him vulnerable? Someone to root for? The writer needs to think about portraying him as a dynamic character. As is, this comes across like a story with low stakes, and one that's maybe a bit too self-consciously clever.

9. One joke in a bio strikes a good balance.
10. I'd avoid ending a query on a question. Gatekeepers know what to do if they want more. Instead, thank them for their consideration.

YOUNG ADULT QUERY #4 FEEDBACK

A REALLY GOOD example of a lighthearted query for a contemporary story. However, the issue might be that it's *too* lighthearted. I don't get a sense of the character, what his damage is, why he needs a comeback, or what he's going through, really, until all of this talk about "redemption" in the last query meat paragraph. Until then, he's a casual dude trying to score. While that's all fine and good, a low-stakes novel that's light on plot does not make for a compelling pitch in the challenging contemporary YA marketplace.

With so many trade books skewing "high-concept," stories without an obvious Hollywood premise need to focus even more on plot and presenting themselves as being otherwise compelling. Is this a romcom? A gut punch/profound journey of self-actualization? The query meat doesn't contain a lot of plot, alas.

The writer spends time describing Colby's situation in a more general way, as a list. The story doesn't start coming together into something linear until after the query midpoint, and even then, some pretty important elements are lumped into another list. Consider this article:

"Query Letter Plot Pitch: Premise vs Plot"

YOUNG ADULT QUERY #5 / HISTORICAL (224 WORDS)

DEAR AWESOME AGENT,

(Personalized greeting, then ...) Complete at 87,000 words, JOLENE is a historical adventure set in the late 1870s about a smart, gutsy Tennessee farm girl who survives by her wits[1] and searches for a place to call home[2].

Abandoned by her Mama and Pa, Jolene believes she's found a home with her Tennessee kin. That is, until Uncle Leroy gets in a fix for money and trades her to lowdown saloonkeeper "King" Ray to pay a debt. But this spirited fifteen-year-old won't be traded[3] off like a farm animal. [With just the clothes on her back and a knife in her boot, she runs][4].

Traveling alone on the Cherokee Trail, Jolene is kidnapped by conmen with unsavory designs, escapes with the help of a kindly Indian and [finds safety with unlikely allies, including a Yankee woman who helps her develop her talents][5]. Just when she thinks she's found her place in the world, King Ray's[6] henchman hunts her down. When he turns up dead, all eyes point to Jolene for murder. [With the evidence stacked up against her, Jolene needs a miracle to keep her from hanging][7].

I am a member of SCBWI, the Historical Novel Society, Women Who Write and two writing critique groups.

[I'd be happy to send you all or part of my manuscript upon request][8]. **Please note that this is a simultaneous submission.** Thank you very much for your consideration.

Sincerely,

(Signature)

---

1. This sounds good, but it's vague. Is this merely a story of bodily survival in a tough environment, or is there another antagonizing force that makes our heroine prove her mettle?
2. A bit of confusion here, too. If she's pitched as a "farm girl," that identity is usually very much tied to place. But she's searching for home. The two don't seem to square. The writer could put more specific information here. I fully expect there to be more detail in the query meat, but loglines can carry context, too.
3. Avoid word repetition in close proximity. See the underlined instances and rephrase.
4. Great! She's in quite the pickle. This also sets her up as a strong protagonist who doesn't just blow in the wind. She takes control (as much as is possible).
5. This starts to get into a list and could flesh out some specific plot points instead. It's also a long sentence. Queries are meant to be read quickly. Maybe think about breaking this up.
6. Is it "King" Ray or King Ray? Keep this consistent throughout the query, as both are currently used.
7. Great! An example of a cliffhanger query. If the writer wanted to go a step further, they'd reveal how Jolene is ultimately triumphant (or not). This will give agents and publishers a sense of the writer's flair for plotting.
8. This is nice, but I'm guessing there are submission guidelines that request at least something. *Tell them* what's included instead.

YOUNG ADULT QUERY #5 FEEDBACK

A NICE AND simple query letter that establishes the character, puts the character in hot water, and ends on a cliffhanger. While I often recommend revealing the ending, this works because it wouldn't be a Western historical without a showdown! The only big note is that I'd like more specifics about the middle of the story and Jolene's journey on the trail. Consider this article:

"Query Letter Plot Pitch: Premise vs Plot"

Does this Yankee woman play into the story in a big way? The character is introduced but dropped. The potential downside of this type of story is that the writer seemingly has the protagonist wandering around alone for long periods of time and responding to random outside attacks (which is passive, meaning the character is reactive instead of proactive). So if there's a central relationship or more of a solid story core in the middle that really challenges Jolene or shapes who she is, I want to know about it.

The pitch doesn't specifically mention that this is YA, either, which leaves it open-ended. It could be adult fiction, which sometimes features teen main characters. I had to double-check with the writer whether this was a YA or adult pitch, and they confirmed it as YA.

However, they also said that it could potentially be good for upper middle grade or adult.

This is an error in judgment. Always pick a category. Here, the protagonist is too old for middle grade, so it'd be a fit for YA or adult fiction. Making a focused choice about the target category at this phase will inform this writer's agent and publisher research and decision-making. Don't leave this crucial element up in the air.

YOUNG ADULT QUERY #6 / SCI-FI (390 WORDS)

DEAR AGENT,

THE FUTURE'S QUEEN is a completed 70,000-word [young adult science fiction romance novel][1]. [Though this book can stand alone, I've begun work on the sequel with the working title, THE FORGOTTEN'S QUEEN][2].

Seventeen-year-old Cesa (Princess) Zamaya of the Kingdom of Navar is a reluctant future reina[3] (queen). But who could blame **her?**[4] **[Her** betrothed might be a murderer and her own mother wants her dead][5].

Planet Nibiru has been divided into quarters. Genetically enhanced royalty governs each quarter[6]. The royalty of Navar have forged an alliance with the Kingdom of Sirian to take dominion of the northern hemisphere with Zamaya's marriage. But there are two problems. 1) Zamaya is not like other royals. She has emotions and feels compassion for her kingdom. 2) Zamaya refuses to marry the cipe (prince). She knows if her mother discovers this weakness and her noncompliance[7], Zamaya won't see her eighteenth birthday.

[To escape her royal prison and impending death, Zamaya unknowingly puts herself into the arms of a pirate who plans to sell her to one of the royal families of the southern quarters to prevent a war that could destroy the planet][8]. Zamaya's safety, [and ascension to the throne are only further complicated by][9] her growing feelings for the [pirate, who is a very powerful being trying to take over the planet for his own species][10]. Ultimately, **Zamaya has to choose** ~~the choice Zamaya has to make is~~[11] between honor, accepting her role as queen ~~by marrying her betrothed~~[12], and her love for the pirate who betrays her.

[As an educator in an urban school district in Kansas, I wanted to write this book to represent a hero and heroine in a science fiction novel that illustrates the vast diversity I'm so privileged to work with daily][13]. After receiving my MFA in Writing Popular Fiction at Seton Hill University, I wanted to[14] query my thesis novel and begin my career as a professional writer.

After reviewing your #MSWL and website, I was excited to query an agent who shares my passion for YA and believes in the importance of diverse sci-fi and fantasy novels. [I believe this novel is a great fit for what you are looking to represent][15].

Included, you will find the first ten pages of my novel and my synopsis. **Please note that this is a simultaneous submission.** I appreciate your time and consideration. I look forward to hearing from you soon.

Thank you,

(Signature)

---

1. For projects that have multiple category and genre elements, the writer will want to consider the order. This phrasing tells me that it's more sci-fi than romance. If that's wrong, then "romantic sci-fi" or "romance with science fiction elements" is more appropriate. If it's more sci-fi than anything else, then "science fiction with romantic elements" or this writer's existing phrasing works, too.
2. This screams that it's not actually a standalone and the writer fully intends a sequel. I would avoid crashing the focus of the query right in the first paragraph by discussing (and naming!) another manuscript. Focus on pitching one book first, then discuss future books if there's initial interest. This puts the cart before the horse.
3. This is Spanish. Is there a Spanish culture or language element, or is the writer creating their own fantasy novums (which just so happen to be Spanish)?
4. Break up this sentence.

5. This sounds great, but I'd go a bit further into *why*, rather than simply dropping this information.
6. Avoid word repetition in close proximity. See the underlined instances and rephrase.
7. "Noncompliance" is a rather dry word for the category. "Rebellion" or similar might have more emotional juice. Is this why Mom wants her dead? That element is still vague. Also, it seems strange that Mom doesn't know what Zamaya has feelings or empathy. How did a kid manage to hide this for almost eighteen years?
8. Good stuff, but a lot for one sentence. Try to break this up.
9. Dry voice. I'd like to see the writer try again with cleaner, smoother language. Especially for YA.
10. Maybe clarify earlier that he's not from the planet. In this world, why is that a problem? Be specific.
11. My changes attempt to make this less wordy.
12. Implied at this point.
13. Good stuff but the sentence is very long.
14. The past tense here is odd. The writer "wanted to"? What happened? Then it becomes clear that this manuscript is, indeed, the thesis. This phrasing could be streamlined.
15. Could omit. This sounds a bit generic and doesn't fit as true personalization.

YOUNG ADULT QUERY #6 FEEDBACK

THERE ARE nice elements to this query that deal with setting up the main character's situation. But the writer should keep in mind that the "royal prison" they reference (a character trapped in their role) is a very common trope. I'd insert a sentence that specifically addresses how this story is different, phrased as part of the pitch. For example, "This take on the timeless royal prison idea unfolds against the backdrop of a dynamic intergalactic world ..." This approach makes it sound desirable ("timeless"!) and like the writer has considered their market angle.

The elements introduced in the very beginning of the query (the mother wanting Zamaya dead and a fiancé who's a murderer) seem a bit bait-and-switch here because the writer doesn't follow up on them by the end of the letter, especially on the murderer.

If these elements are mentioned in the logline, they should gather resonance in the query meat. As is, these points are left dangling.

The voice could use a bit of work, too. The writer has some long, complex sentences and wordy phrasing. Especially as an MFA creative writing graduate in the very voice-driven YA category, this writer will be held to high standards. Voice problems in the query don't bode well for the manuscript itself, so the writer won't want to cast doubt on their own abilities.

YOUNG ADULT QUERY #7 / FANTASY (291 WORDS)

Dear Properly-Spelled-Agent's-Name[1],

Based on your interest in X, I thought you might like my YA fantasy, BENEATH THE VIOLET, complete at about 85,000 words.

[The inhabitants of Chartown live under a perpetual violet fog: it's just the way of things, as much a part of life as the cobblestones beneath their feet or the fact that everyone has their own particular magic power][2].

Except one girl. Tess Dawkins has a secret shared only with her two closest friends: unlike everyone **else** ~~she knows~~, she has no power at all. She's also a Guff[3]: a poor orphan who scrounges for dinner in the trash alleys and fends for herself on the city streets. With only weeks left until her eighteenth birthday, [she must conjure a strong power][4] or risk conscription to the labor camps, never to see her friends again.

~~So~~ **W**hen[5] Tess finds a book in the trash that speaks of the powerless, she hopes it may lead to her missing power. Instead, the book's clues, and [the help of a young soldier],[6] catapult her into the world of the elites. [There she becomes the pawn of a calculating Vice Admiral who would tip the balance of power from the Lords to the Admiralty][7].

Only her ability to pretend, [honed by years of faking a power, can keep her alive][8]. But as she learns the truth about her city and its violet skies, staying alive is no longer enough. [The elites have plans to control her world's every breath][9]. Powerless as she may be, it's up to Tess to stop them.

BENEATH THE VIOLET is THE RED QUEEN meets THE SHIP BREAKER: environmental themes, class exploitation, and girl power in a world of technology[10] and magic. It's a stand-alone with potential for a sequel.

(Bio Paragraph)

Please find the first XYZ pages pasted below, per your guidelines. This is a simultaneous submission. Thank you very much for your consideration!

Sincerely,

(Signature)

---

1. Ha!
2. Some nice writing (the "perpetual violet fog" and "cobblestones" details are atmospheric and set the mood) but this writer is burying the fantasy hook at the end of a long sentence. Remember, with fantasy and other high-concept pitches, agents and publishers are always wondering what makes them unique. This "everyone has their own particular magic power" is the fantasy element. But the reader will be tired from the nice but unessential details by the time they reach this concrete tidbit.
3. Does she need two big secrets? This is obviously a premise question, not a query one, but both don't really factor into the pitch. Can one be enough?
4. Is this up to her? If so, why hasn't she done it already? I like the high stakes phrasing here, but the query also makes it seem like her problem has a solution ... so why isn't this something Tess has tried already? Or is the implication here that she has to do the impossible?
5. I'd start with "When" here. "So" is a bit too chatty.
6. This seems very randomly mentioned in the middle of a sentence about the book. Is there another way to introduce the soldier?
7. World politics suddenly come into play in a big way. But these words mean very little to me. The writer would do well to add context. What are the stakes? Why is this important? Why is this bad or good?
8. This is already well established, so I'm not sure this explanation is necessary.
9. This sounds nice and dramatic, but I'm not sure what this actually means in plot terms, or how it ties to magic.
10. If there's a sci-fi element, work that genre into the pitch somehow.

YOUNG ADULT QUERY #7 FEEDBACK

A STRONG FANTASY QUERY, but one that could do more in terms of solidifying the worldbuilding. Especially the political elements of the larger society involved, which don't come into play until the final paragraph of the meat. (The first two paragraphs of the meat focus exclusively on the magic powers—or lack thereof—and how they affect the protagonist.)

Things suddenly change in the third meat paragraph with the introduction of many new elements. The writer should either plant seeds for these developments earlier, or take more time with them by offering additional context. 50 more words wouldn't hurt the overall length. Otherwise, this query has strong comps and nice stakes, though the writer could always make them more specific. Consider this article:

"Concrete Writing: Using Specific Language"

Finally, there is some solid, atmospheric writing in the opening. It does distract from the main fantasy hook because of an overlong sentence, but it also sets the tone. However, it largely disappears after that initial flourish. If the writer wants to set themselves apart with voice or writing style in the query, they should do more throughout. Fading in and out calls attention to the voice, and maybe for the wrong reasons.

A lot of queries introduce elements, then drop them. Ideally, the things mentioned early in a logline or query meat will be brought back around by the end of the pitch.

This is emerging as a leading note on many of these examples. Think of the query as an interconnected ecosystem. Is yours in balance? Or are certain elements dangling and disconnected?

YOUNG ADULT QUERY #8 / MULTIPLE POV (336 WORDS)

(Writer Address)

(Date)

(Agent Address)[1]

Dear Ms. Doe,

[After reading Talley Fredrick's *Girls Aflame* and Katie Marshall's *Girls Made of Fire*, I'm contacting you as a potential fit for representation][2]. [I hope this query will interest you][3] in my ~~60k~~ **60,000-word**[4] YA novel, YOU ARE HERE.

Maria Santana Silverman lives in one world—her mother's bohemian San Francisco where she's constantly **labeled—and** dreams of **another —her**[5] father's affluent Beverly Hills [where labels are everything][6]. Is she Catholic or Jewish? Latina or White? Poor or rich? Idealist or pragmatic? [Debate, where labels don't matter, is the one place she feels powerful][7].

Like water, Claire Lefevre submits to the shape of the labels that contain her: Old Money. Tennis Star. Barbie Doll. Initially, boarding school is a refuge from her sterile Boca Raton home life. Dating the school's most popular guy[8] [is a chance for connection and reinvention][9]. But she won't fix her anxiety until she figures out who she really is and creates her own label.

Erin O'Malley classifies herself by a label that's as straightforward as she is: a botany-obsessed scientist from Idaho farm country. She loves her close-knit family but feels pressured to take over their business[10] instead of going to college. [Pulling up deep roots and replanting herself makes the decision to leave her family, and her first love, even harder][11].

These three very different young women—for three different reasons—have the same dream: to make it to ~~the~~ prestigious Sherman College. The book culminates in Maria, Claire and Erin's meeting. [They find in each other a reflection and affirmation that they are all survivors—and thrivers, the architects of their lives. Living together is the best chance for them to chart their own course, even if they ~~themselves~~ don't know it yet][12].

My children's content has been published by Universal Kids, PBSKids and *Seventeen*. I'm a SCBWI picture book winner and RUCCL-invitee with degrees in Children's Media from Brown and Columbia.

Thank you for your time and consideration. **The first XYZ pages are pasted below. Please note that this is a simultaneous submission.** I look forward to hearing from you at: (Email) or (Phone Number)[13].

Kindly,

(Signature)

Enclosed: YOU ARE HERE (first ten pages)[14]

---

1. Feel free to skip these holdovers from letter writing for an email query.
2. Good personalization.
3. This goes without saying. Play with phrasing that maybe combines "I'm contacting you ..." with this. We don't need both.
4. Put the number, not "60k."
5. I'd opt for em-dashes here instead of commas. Also, this is quite a long sentence for the query opening. I worry that it's work to read, especially as an entry into the document.

6. The sentence states that she is in World A but dreams of World B. In World A, she's "constantly labeled." This would suggest that World B might be an escape from labels. But in World B, "labels are everything." So in terms of labels, World A and World B are the same. Where's the friction?
7. Now the writer is saying that World C (debate) is where she actually wants to be. So which is it? Does she dream of World B or C? I can see where the writer is going with the set-up for this paragraph but I worry about the logic.
8. Isn't "popular guy," ironically, a label, though?
9. This paragraph doesn't give me a clear sense that she hates her labels, necessarily, so the conflict seems fuzzy.
10. Because of the rural setting, I'm wondering if the family business has to do with agriculture. If this is the case, wouldn't a botanist want to stick around?
11. A bit of awkward phrasing here.
12. The query doesn't give a sense of dire straits for any of the girls. So the term "survivors" seems odd here. They are all dealing with identity, which is a good theme for YA, but I don't have a sense that the stakes are quite this high.
13. This information should appear below the signature.
14. Also a holdover from formal letter writing.

YOUNG ADULT QUERY #8 FEEDBACK

THE CHALLENGE of a multiple POV query letter is demonstrated here. A query writer's job is to sell the reader on a compelling story. In this example, the writer has *three* characters to cover. Unfortunately, the writer has only been able to present each character's baseline situation, really—and in some cases, in pretty vague terms. By then, the clock is ticking to tie everything together.

I'd be sure to mention right from the beginning, also, that this manuscript is multiple POV, and maybe how the narrative combines these perspectives. Are the girls' stories interwoven, or are there basically three novellas until the characters get to college and collide? Any time a writer uses a different storytelling style, that's relevant information for the agent or publisher to know right away.

In specific query terms, this writer is perhaps limiting themselves with their focus on labels. I get it. It's a good organizing principle, and the topic of identity is thematically rich for YA. However, it sets the writer up to just deliver a list about each character without focusing on concrete plot. Why is Erin leaving home, for example? Why does Claire want to reinvent herself when she's actually described as adhering to her labels? Reinvent herself in response to … what? Knowing the characters' backstory is important, but this is merely set-up. The letter neglects to spend much time on what happens in the present moment, it seems.

If this was my query, I'd focus on each girl's external conflict as much —if not more—than their internal conflict (which is where the writer currently spends most of their time). That way, when the writer calls the three young women "survivors" in the "everything comes together" paragraph, it feels more earned. As is, I don't see anything here that they are surviving, other than the exploration of their identities, so that high-stakes term doesn't ring true.

Dive more deeply into plot. Otherwise, an agent or publisher might think that we have three teen girls navel-gazing and then coming together to do more of the same. That's definitely not what this writer wants to convey, even unintentionally.

The college setting is also potentially problematic. Most YA novels feature characters who are between sixteen and eighteen years old, and take place before the protagonist leaves home (with some exceptions). Has the writer considered pitching this as New Adult, which takes readers to college and beyond? That's a smaller market, but the character ages might be a better fit for this category.

YOUNG ADULT QUERY #9 / CONTEMPORARY (330 WORDS)

DEAR MS. / MR. Amazing Literary Agent,

Fifteen-year-old[1] Meghan Lane is left everything when her grandmother dies: [the family castle, an enchanted forest, and orders to solve a mystery involving a pack of wolves accused of mauling a young boy][2].

Meghan is suspicious, especially when she discovers her grandmother faked her death using the magic that's been part of the family since the beginning of time. [Magic that Meghan knew nothing about—until she accessed the forest when no ordinary citizen could. When Meghan unwittingly exhibits her power, her grandmother recruits her to join **the** Guardians of the Wild][3]—protectors of Earth against the Death Sorcerer[4]—[to help her out of a major magic mess that she created][5].

[Zach Fisher's new friendship with Meghan results in his losing consciousness][6]. Multiple times. [Not the best way to build trust][7]. His wariness of her worsens[8] when he learns that Meghan and her grandmother are using magic to [protect the pack of wolves accused of mauling his little brother][9]. When Meghan explains that they think the wolves might be innocent, Zach must decide between trusting his memory and [trusting the girl whose touch makes him black out and manipulates his thoughts][10].

The mystery behind Zach's brother's death drives Zach and Meghan together in a clash of opposition[11]. Zach believes what he remembers[12], and Meghan believes his memory isn't real. One thing they do agree on: [they have no idea if the Guardians of the Wild are the good guys or the bad guys][13].

Determined to uncover the truth, Zach and Meghan strike an uneasy truce and work together. If they can't prove the wolves are innocent, [then Meghan's grandmother will be accused of murderous witchcraft, and the Guardians of the Wild will be unveiled—risking the only protection the natural world has against the Death Sorcerer][14].

But it's hard to argue gnawed human bones.

TWO SISTERS WOODS is a YA Contemporary Fantasy with series potential, complete at 74,000 words.

I am published in (writing credits)[15].

Please find the first XYZ pages pasted below, per your guidelines. Note that this is a simultaneous submission. Thank you for your time and consideration.

(Signature)

---

1. This is a bit of a gray area for YA. Most YA characters are sixteen to eighteen because readers like to "read up" about characters slightly older than they are, and fifteen is considered young for YA.
2. This query does start with a list, but I'm compelled immediately because the list is unexpected. The last element (the wolves) provides conflict right away.
3. So is her magic that she can go into the enchanted forest, or is there more to it? Fantasy is a crowded category. Be sure to be very specific about the fantasy element.
4. I'd also like to know more about this, what this is, what its mission is, what the stakes are. The writer should add more context in this paragraph, or the next one.
5. Too vague. What about the mauling mystery? This seems forgotten. I want to know about this mess more, because Meghan seems to have a direct connection to it (more so than some random kid getting mauled). The female pronouns are also confusing, as the writer talks about Meghan and Grandma here, and I'm not sure who "she" is and who "her" refers to.

6. An abrupt shift. Is this a dual POV project? If so, make that clear up top in the logistical paragraph.
7. *Are* they trying to build trust, though? They seem to firmly dislike one another, so why would they want to get on better terms?
8. A roundabout way of getting here. Why is he wary of her?
9. Ah. Gotcha. But now I'm doubly confused. If Grandma's fake death tasks Meghan with solving the mauling mystery (per the first paragraph), why are Meghan and Grandma now protecting the wolves? These two ideas seem contradictory.
10. The blacking out element could be much clearer in this paragraph. This is the first we're hearing of thought manipulation (a magic?), and I feel like it needs to be introduced more directly.
11. This phrasing is redundant. "Clash" and "opposition" are similar.
12. Restating a bit from the previous paragraph.
13. This sounds good. But why? They're mentioned, but they haven't come into the story pitch at all.
14. These elements aren't coming together for me just yet, least of all the Death Sorcerer. See the feedback chapter.
15. Writing credits are a great thing to include in a bio paragraph, but I wonder whether there's anything else the writer might mention. It's possible to be too professional, at the expense of the personal.

YOUNG ADULT QUERY #9 FEEDBACK

THIS IS A WELL-WRITTEN QUERY, but the presentation of the story itself is confusing. Are these events going to be told in dual POV, or are we primarily in Meghan's experience? Why are the wolves such a big deal to her family? (I can tell why they matter to Zach, obviously, but not how wolves, Meghan, and Grandma collide.) Why is Grandma faking her death and then being accused of murder? This makes her seem obviously guilty and takes tension away from the mystery.

What, exactly, is the magic they use? What are the Guardians of the Wild, and why are they either good or bad? What's the mess Meghan created? Or is it Grandma's mess? And, last but not least, who's the Death Sorcerer? They have been name-dropped without any further context.

I did gather that there was a mauling. It matters to Meghan (for some reason). It matters to Zach. Meghan has family magic. Zach and Meghan don't agree. Zach is blacking out (for some reason), and this gets a lot of attention in the query (for some reason). I'm afraid this is not enough to help me feel anchored in the story. All of these elements have been presented but aren't coming together. I think the current query sounds good ("But it's hard to argue gnawed human bones" has undeniable pizzazz) but is light on substance and plot logic.

I'd recommend that the writer take a big step back and start over with a two- or three-sentence description of the story, focusing on the role of magic in this world, the Guardians, and the Death Sorcerer. Then layer in the adversarial relationship between Zach and Meghan. Then the wolf/Grandma conflict. Finally, bring it all together with how Meghan's personal magic fits into everything.

But without the worldbuilding logic, it might be very tough for a gatekeeper to get a foothold in this pitch, and that's a query letter liability.

YOUNG ADULT QUERY #10 (339 WORDS)

Received Representation and a Book Deal!

Dear Agent,

[If being a math nerd with an odd affection for calculators wasn't enough to make Eva Walker a high school misfit, her aversion to touch has pretty much sealed her fate][1]. But she can't help it~~:~~ **W**henever she lays a hand on anyone or their stuff, she gets haunting and unwelcome glimpses into their issues, from majorly messed-up childhoods to simple struggles with calculus. So Eva has learned to keep her hands to herself—[not exactly where teenage boys want a girl's hands][2].

Having baffled doctors and psychic healers alike, Eva knows her last hope for a normal life (and maybe a boyfriend she can touch someday) [is to put her nerdiness to good use, study neuroscience, and try to cure herself].[3] But given her family's size and less-than-stellar financial situation, she needs a scholarship. A BIG one.

To make extra money (and, to be honest, for fun) she tutors the mathematically challenged**. When** she lets her guard down and touches Zenn Bennett's old army jacket, ~~the~~ a dark and violent vision literally knocks her off her feet. But Eva can't resist a challenge … or a talented artist and troubled fellow loner **who's**[4] absolutely irresistible without trying at all. Eva's feelings intensify when she discovers that, his jacket aside, Zenn is the only person she can touch without having visions. [But when they end up competing for the same huge scholarship that could be the key to either of them going to college, their relationship hits a snag][5]. [And that's nothing compared to when they find out exactly why his jacket haunts her, and how their lives were permanently tangled together long before they ever met][6].

ZENN DIAGRAM is my 72,000-word YA contemporary novel with a slight touch of the paranormal—think [*Frozen* meets John Green][7]. I believe it would appeal to a similar audience as Lauren Oliver's *Before I Fall*. My writing credentials include a degree in journalism from Northwestern University and completion of the University of Denver's Publishing Institute.

I've pasted the first XYZ pages below, per your guidelines. Please note that this is a simultaneous submission. Thank you for your consideration.

Sincerely,

(Signature)

---

1. I'd argue that this is a bit wordy. There are a lot of attributes listed here. Give them some room to breathe. What's most important? Putting everything in a list makes it tough to tell. Is it that she's a nerd or that she doesn't like to be touched? If it's the latter, burying it at the end of a long sentence downplays its importance.
2. The wordiness dilutes the humor a bit. Keep jokes short and punchy, e.g., "not exactly what teen boys want."
3. Good. Strong objective here. And high stakes. She's out of options, and she wants a fix for this problem. Also, the writer should make sure it's clear that she wants to study neuroscience *in college,* as this will come up in a moment. Otherwise, this could be interpreted as her simply researching it on her own.
4. I recommend contractions whenever possible.
5. Great, the urgency behind her financial stake in the story is clear. I like that the writer does a good job of making Zenn both compelling to her but a potential conflict. He has a dark past, and he's competition.
6. There's enough substance on the page about the plot already that I don't mind this cliffhanger here.
7. An oddball comp, but it does make me want to know more.

YOUNG ADULT QUERY #10 FEEDBACK

A STRONG NOVEL QUERY, and no wonder! This query got an offer of rep, and the project went on to score a book deal! What I admire the most here is the clear presentation of a compelling character who has a big problem. She can't touch anyone. And she's a nerd. Now she must use her powers to try and solve her problem, but family issues and finances get in the way. Her path crosses with a dark, mysterious boy's. He also has a secret.

The writer is hitting a lot of YA category tropes here. The only thing that I wish was woven into the later query meat is a sense of whether Eva's touching "talent" (or curse?) is somehow connected to her and Zenn's mysterious bond. It seems that way, since she can touch him without getting her visions. But maybe if that was made clearer in the query, it would bring the focus on her power full-circle. This query also takes a risk with the comp. *Frozen* meets John Green? Huh? How does *that* work? Well, the flashes of humor in the query, as well as a strong overall pitch, make me intrigued rather than confused.

If a writer takes some calculated risks in their letter, as long as the other elements work well, agents or publishers may well be willing to go out on a limb. In this case, it has paid off!

Nonfiction Queries

NONFICTION QUERY #1 / PICTURE BOOK (293 WORDS)

RECEIVED REPRESENTATION AND A BOOK DEAL!

(DATE)

(Agent Address)[1]

Dear Ms. Sonnack,

[I've followed your sales and interests for quite some time and noted your recent tweet about your daughter wanting to be a scientist. I have a perfect role model for her—Dr. Virginia Apgar][2]. My PB biography, ~~of Dr. Apgar:~~ [BREATHE, BABY, BREATHE: HOW DR. VIRGINIA APGAR'S SCORE SAVED MILLIONS OF BABIES (AND STILL DOES)][3]**, shares her story.**

Born in 1909, Virginia Apgar overcame social pressures, lack of resources, and gender bias to become a doctor, scientist, teacher and inventor. She is most known for inventing the APGAR Score, a test given to every baby born in a hospital around the world. It is the first and most important test we take, [because it quickly determines the health of a baby and if that baby needs immediate medical attention][4]. Invented in 1949, it is still the determinate[5] for newborn health.

Before Dr. Apgar invented the APGAR Score, babies who couldn't breathe, were premature, or otherwise compromised were often set aside to die. Virginia used her unwavering fortitude, charisma, and intelligence to change this practice and revolutionize neonatal and newborn care.

[Surprisingly, Dr. Apgar's life and/or accomplishments haven't been explored in a picture book][6]. She **was** included in two anthologies and in 2004, she was the subject of a Rosen Women Hall of Famers in Mathematics and Science series. This completed biography would reinforce discussions around women in STEM, medicine, and history as well as encourage all children to pursue their dreams.

I am the author of two science/nature picture books with Arbordale and a NF PB releasing in (publishing season) with Charlesbridge. I am the SCBWI Michigan co-Regional Advisor and a former early childhood teacher. I also have experience as a solopreneur in business development and marketing.

You can find the complete manuscript pasted below. Please note that this is a simultaneous submission. I look forward to hearing from you.

Warmly,

(Signature)

---

1. These are holdovers from letter formatting. You don't really need them for a query letter intended for email. (This looks fancy, but that's about it.)
2. To take such a personal approach could be a risk (sounding creepy is never a good look for a query, especially when it comes to mentioning an agent or editor's private life), but this writer pulls it off perfectly! There really is a personal (but not *too* personal) tie-in here!
3. I've rearranged this a bit so that the subject's name isn't repeated.
4. This is crucial but gets lost at the end of a long sentence. I'd consider breaking this up.
5. There's some dry voice here, even though this is technically a science pitch. But it's a science pitch for kid readers, so voice is a factor when it otherwise wouldn't matter

as much (e.g., in an academic paper). "Gold standard for determining" or "determining factor" or similar would be less formal.

6. After the writer sells me on such an important idea, this comes across as surprising, too. The picture book nonfiction market loves "undiscovered" stories, so this is a huge sales hook.

NONFICTION QUERY #1 FEEDBACK

An awesome nonfiction picture book query letter. And you can tell, because it got an offer of representation and has become *Virginia Wouldn't Slow Down!: The Unstoppable Dr. Apgar and Her Life-Saving Invention*, from Norton. The picture book nonfiction market thrives on undiscovered stories or new, fresh angles on familiar events and people. So this really hits the sweet spot, first by introducing me to Virginia Apgar (everyone who's ever had a baby has heard of the APGAR score, after all) and then surprising me with the idea that there's no book about her yet. Finally, the timing for this project couldn't be more perfect, as publisher and reader interest in women in STEAM has hit an all-time high.

Concept aside, the query has mastered the subtle art of creating a need and then fulfilling it. This is crucial in nonfiction because the sales hook and the potential market for a project are going to be top considerations for agents and publishers. Maybe before the market awakened to a need to champion female doctors, scientists, inventors, and engineers, Apgar's story would've been considered too niche, but not anymore. This entire project is lightning striking at the right time, in the right place, and with a great pitch, to boot.

NONFICTION QUERY #2 / BUSINESS (166 WORDS)

DEAR AGENT,

[Business professionals are not yet "literate" in video communication and web conferencing][1]. However, online video is being used to communicate, teach, inform, sell, and more. [Video is quickly becoming the new dominant medium for business communication][2]. My nonfiction book, *On-Camera Pro,* [teaches professionals how to effectively conduct business via video and how to present on camera with impact][3].

As a writer with expertise in multimedia and technology, I am seeking representation from an agent who shares my same passion. [Your interest in multimedia and technology is apparent from your website and social media presence][4]. [Your track record for representing award-winning books is impressive as well. I would greatly welcome the opportunity to work with you][5].

I have ~~also~~ published several articles in [professional trade association journals][6] related to business video and video communication. [Given the recent explosion of online video, on-camera tips and techniques for effective communication would appeal to business professionals globally][7].

Please find my book proposal pasted below, per your guidelines. This is a simultaneous submission. Thank you for your consideration.

Looking forward to hearing from you,

(Signature)

---

1. Good. This creates a perceived problem. However, the writer would do well to make the problem more dire. Why is this a big issue? What kind of benefit would business professionals enjoy if they became more video-literate? This statement is a good starting point, but I would've expected more of an "And? So?" to help drive it home. Obviously, this query was attempted and workshopped before business went remote, so I'd say this writer made some good predictions. If this idea was being pitched post-pandemic, though, I'd spend less time explaining the need for video. The entire project needs a bit of a pivot.
2. Some concrete facts here, with citations, would really do wonders for the pitch. For example, "According to a PEW Research study, 94% of business is now conducted via video chat ..." or similar. Obviously, this is a made-up statistic, but a real and compelling one, if it exists, would bolster the argument. Otherwise, phrases like "not yet" and "quickly becoming the new dominant medium" sound good, but I'm wondering, "Says who? What is this writer basing their arguments on?" In a nonfiction project, data bolsters credibility.
3. The writer could add an entire new paragraph here to go into more detail about the book's contents. See the feedback chapter.
4. Hmm, this is a bit of a tangential connection. Most agents will have websites and social media presence. That does not imply, at least to me, an automatic interest in web and social media.
5. This "personalization" seems generic. A specific title referenced here would make it sing. Otherwise, this could be said of anyone. Also, is "award-winning" the most relevant criteria here? The book that's being pitched is extremely utilitarian, but is it award fodder?
6. Be specific about the titles here. Is the writer also affiliated with those trade associations as a video/media professional?
7. This restates the first paragraph and I'm not sure it offers anything new.

NONFICTION QUERY #2 FEEDBACK

Nonfiction queries, when done right, need to accomplish three things:

1. Establish a market need for the book;
2. Pitch why the book in question will fill this need and how;
3. Convince the reader that the writer is *the* expert on the topic will do all of the above.

This query does points one and three pretty well, but could do more. For example, concrete numbers to support the explosion of business being done via video would go a long way in terms of creating a perceived need for point one. Publications and trade association names, as well as relevant work experience in video/media communication, would help establish the writer's credibility for point three.

The biggest opportunity for growth is point two. From the sentence, "teaches professionals how to effectively conduct business via video and how to present on camera with impact," I don't get a strong sense of what the book will actually be. It sounds like a list of tips. Well, that's better known as an article. (Or a listicle, if you want to get technical.) Every single nonfiction agent or editor is going to be asking themselves the following question: "Does this have enough juice for a book, or is this a glorified article?"

Here, there isn't a lot to convince me that an article couldn't adequately cover the topic. So what, exactly, is going to be the book-worthy substance of this, if published? How are we going to get 250 pages of content? A brand new paragraph of specific examples of the project's substance would help allay these concerns.

Consider this article (though the project being pitched here is not a children's book, the point holds firm that sometimes there's enough content for a book, and sometimes there isn't):

"Nonfiction Children's Book vs. Article"

Finally, the sea change of video communication for business has already arrived in the years since the pitch was written. Now, I'd recommend that the writer find the pain points that emerged during the world's remote work experiment from 2019 to 2022, and lean into how a professional video strategy could address them going forward.

Memoir Query

MEMOIR QUERY #1 / MIDDLE GRADE (349 WORDS)

Received Representation and a Book Deal!

Dear Ms. Cummings,

[We would like to introduce you to our middle grade creative nonfiction story, *The Year of the Buttered Cat*][1].

A bizarre medical error days after her birth has left thirteen-year-old Lexi unable to walk or talk and with wildly erratic muscle control. [Although she has zero desire to be like everyone else—after all, she has some incredible gifts she wouldn't trade for anything—she *does* need a voice][2]. Six years ago, she endured an experimental brain surgery in hopes it would help her speak. That surgery wasn't a slam dunk, but it gave her a glimmer of hope and the courage to try again.

Now, Lexi is a thousand miles from home and counting down the hours to a second surgery when she [receives a mysterious message][3] —"Why on earth would you put her through this again?" But this **second surgery is**[4] *Lexi's* choice—*her* brain, *her* decision. The audacity of the question motivates Lexi to tell her story. She plunges into her past, dovetailing her current countdown to surgery with the story of the Year of the Buttered Cat. That year, Lexi discovered what happened to her as a baby and what it meant for her future and her family. It was also the year she discovered[5] the five gifts that would help her navigate life[6].

Lexi is confident about her decision to undergo a second surgery until she's blindsided by an unexpected complication that threatens to steal her gifts. Now, she is left with the impossible task of deciding if gaining her voice is worth the risk[7] of losing the precious gifts that define her.

The Year of the Buttered Cat is complete at 47,500 words. It is based on a true story and is co-written by Lexi. We believe it would appeal to fans of Palacio's *Wonder* (albeit a bit older) and Haddon's *The Curious Incident of the Dog in the Night-Time.* Susan has been a freelance medical writer for over 20 years and is a member of **the** SCBWI.

This is a simultaneous submission and the full manuscript is available upon request. **The first XYZ pages are pasted below.** Thank you for your consideration.

Sincerely,

(Signature)

---

1. This is maybe a bit too straightforward for a first sentence. I'd recommend adding the word count and maybe some personalization. Use that opening sentence to its full potential. It's the project's big first impression.
2. Really great phrasing here, and this gets to the emotional heart of the story right away.
3. How does the message arrive? This question pulls me out of the query a bit, because not everyone would have access to a thirteen-year-old to send such a message. I'm wondering if the detail about the message is necessary for the purpose of the query, because it doesn't come up again. Maybe just, "But she can't help wondering: why would she do this again if it didn't work the first time?"
4. I think present tense makes more sense here because the majority of the query is in the present timeline.
5. The trick with word echo isn't in reaching for a thesaurus to simply replace the word. It's in looking at the overall syntax to see, "Hey, is there another way I could phrase this sentence so that I don't *have* to repeat myself?"
6. A very strong pitch so far. The project also has an unusual narrative structure that cuts between present and past. That'd be good to mention right away. This should be a consideration for all manuscripts with more unique narrative styles.

7. By the third and fourth mention of gifts, however, I am starting to realize that these gifts are really important to the story, but I have no idea what they are. This part of the query gets a bit vague. I like that the surgery is a double-edged scalpel, if you will, and that it has a potential downside. But if I don't know *what* Lexi is risking (the exact nature of the gifts), then the picture isn't as clear. There's also some repetition here, so the writer should consider streamlining.

MEMOIR QUERY #1 FEEDBACK

THE KEY to creative nonfiction (also called "memoir" or "narrative nonfiction") is the human element. Readers won't be compelled to read about a person whose story they aren't interested in. They also want to glean something for themselves while reading, even if they're not consciously aware of this need to relate. (In this case, it seems that the takeaways for memoir readers will be hope and the inspiration to overcome obstacles.)

Here, Lexi's journey promises a lot of emotion, and the "plot" (I put this in quotes here because this is technically someone's life, but the events are structured more like a story) seems to have the requisite amount of struggle and triumph.

Lexi is, after all, dealing with a medical condition that sounds quite challenging to navigate. And her underlying theme of finding her voice (literally, in this case) is extremely universal for readers of all ages, not just middle grade.

One reason the narrative works here? This project tugs at the heartstrings and makes the risk she's considering (a serious surgery) a compelling decision that I want to read about. So we have a character who readers can root for (as evidenced by glimpses we get into Lexi's attitude and worldview), a big challenge, a unique situation, a big risk and/or decision, and the possibility of triumph. Think about the memoirs you've read, and you will find all or most of these elements present.

The biggest pitfall is that the gifts aren't defined, despite this idea getting repeated several times. I'd rather have context over redundancy. That third paragraph of the query meat needs work, especially since it's the paragraph that will ideally tie everything together. The other tweak I'd make is maybe omitting the detail about the message. It raises more questions than it answers, which is undesirable in a query.

But this letter did well for the co-authors and got them literary representation and a book deal based, I think, on the all-important one-two punch of a strong pitch and a strong story! This memoir became *The Year of the Buttered Cat: A Mostly True Story* from Penelope Editions.

Novel Queries

FICTION QUERY #1 / WOMEN'S FICTION (226 WORDS)

Received Representation and a Book Deal!

A Bonus Letter to Readers[1]

The following query letter was sent to the person who would become my agent. It was sent via snail mail, as that was the preference back then. Although this is the letter that snagged an agent way back in 2009, this specific novel will not be published until the end of 2019. Patience is key in this business!

A query letter is one of the most difficult things to write. It does get easier, but it is still the first bridge between the writer and the agent, and so it is imperative that time and care is taken with the wording.

I have written 14 books in twenty years. Four books are now self-published. Two have won awards. My agent still shops each book that I write, and after a year or so, if it does not sell, he puts it back into my hands to do with as I wish.[2] It is a great symbiotic relationship!

Good luck to all of you as you write your query letters!

The Query Itself

Dear [Agent]:

Thirty-one-year-old Georgia Parks Maclean is a suburban California princess~~:~~. **With** Barbie-blond hair, **she's** lean and beautiful, **a** state college grad~~,~~ **and** mommy wannabe~~,~~ who[3] craves nothing less than the perfect marriage, the perfect beige home, the perfect Montessori babies.

But this façade disintegrates when she discovers something every woman silently fears: Georgia Maclean[4] has breast cancer.

[It will be up to the ghost of Georgia's father, who died on the way to her premature birth],[5] whose face she's only seen in faded newspaper clippings, to guide his daughter through the next few years, from[6] dealing with her husband's acute case of denial, to [convincing her neurotic mother she didn't get cancer just to spite her][7]. [Georgia begins piecing together the scattered fragments of her childhood, **and** unraveling mysteries about the people in her life she hadn't the courage to recognize before][8].

Magical realism [and in-depth research][9] are mingled together in this first-person narrative of a woman who learns that life and love are interchangeable entities.

Like the hit movie *Ghost*, the best-selling novel *She's Come Undone*, or the play *Wit*, my novel *Epiphany* will easily[10] find its way into every woman's psyche. [After reading it, she will have a better perspective of life, love, and the importance of knowing who she is emotionally, physically, spiritually][11].

The ~~ms~~ **manuscript**[12] is 102,000 words and is complete. **Please note that this is a simultaneous submission.** Thank you for your time, consideration, and reply.

Sincerely,

(Signature)

[P.S. I had the pleasure of meeting one-on-one with [Publishing House Editor], at a writer's conference. She handed me her business card and asked that I send the ~~ms~~ **manuscript** via agent only][13].

---

1. This writer was passionate about providing some background and a few words of encouragement! Read on to hear from someone who has been there. A wonderful reminder of the many ways in which a writing career can come together, and how long the process sometimes takes!
2. This working relationship between this writer and their agent sounds great. Some agents only work on books destined for traditional publication. But not every project will have the same path to print (or screen). I love when a writer can see various possibilities for their work and advocate for themselves with their literary representative.
3. I'd make changes along these lines to break up this sentence.
4. There seems to be such pomp about the three-word name earlier. Why not repeat it? It communicates the tone of who she is subtly, so I'd keep it consistent.
5. Interesting! This premise does take a bit of a left turn here with the sudden paranormal (?) focus. If there was a logistical paragraph to the query, the writer might mention a category of "women's fiction with a paranormal element," or similar, to prepare the reader for this. Agents and publishers like to think of book categories right away, so it's the writer's job to help them know where to slot the project.
6. A lot of good stuff going on here. I'd find a way to break this sentence up, though. Too much detail in one sentence can scatter reader focus instead of sharpening it.
7. Ha! A lot of relationship conflict promised.
8. Why is this significant for her and her stated objective of having the perfect life? Maybe tie it back to the first paragraph.
9. On what? Ghosts? Could be clearer.
10. Maybe a bit too much swagger with "easily" and "every" (a big promise!), but I like the comps.
11. This is also a big promise. I might omit this because there's a fine line between thematic analysis and overconfidence, which might set the wrong tone.
12. In "industry speak," "ms" stands for "manuscript." While this writer certainly seems savvy, I'd avoid using only one instance of shorthand in an otherwise polished letter.
13. This is a great note to add in the query if the writer has a "warm lead" on their hands with an editor at a publishing house. It shows that they've been out networking and are professional enough to get in-person requests. Sure, it may not amount to much, or the agent might not want to pitch to that specific editor, but this sends a strong signal that the writer is hard at work generating excitement for the project.

FICTION QUERY #1 FEEDBACK

A GREAT QUERY, and perfect for the women's fiction category. This character had her life all planned out, and then an unexpected event challenges her and forces her to either sink or swim. Her preconceived notions are shattered, and she has to rebuild her sense of self by digging into her past (in this case, with some paranormal help). Self-inquiry and the integration of past and present are popular themes in women's fiction, but this story stands out with the element of Dad's ghost.

The only two notes I'd really give would be to pitch it as "women's fiction with a paranormal element" or "magical realism" (as the writer does later in the query) right in the first paragraph, and to chop up some of those overlong sentences. Otherwise, we get character, we get plot, and we get strong comp titles that make a case for this kind of "helpful ghost" story. It's no wonder that this query got an agent and a contract!

FICTION QUERY #2 / FANTASY (461 WORDS)

DEAR [AGENT]:

DAY WITHOUT DAWN is an epic fantasy with the crossover appeal of [Lani Taylor's *Daughter of Smoke and Bone* and gritty feminism of N. K. Jemisin's *The Hundred Thousand Kingdoms*][1]. It is [complete at 97~~K~~**,000 words** and standalone-capable, yet part of a planned series][2].

[Forged by war, shattered by love,][3] an outcast curses the birthmark that brands her as one of "the blessed" [in a battle to prove she won't betray her adopted nation],[4] that her blood doesn't tell.

[Rejected by her desert tribe for a birthmark which symbolizes their ancient enemy's Mother Goddess,][5] her sire[6] abandons his infant along the A'talan border. Pell a'Sada, an A'talan commander, finds and adopts ~~the child~~ **her**[7] for that same birthmark. Thea's bronze skin and sapphire eyes mark her as his people's hated "other," yet she's allowed to grow up wild and free on the grasslands. A gifted archer and natural on ~~the back of a horse~~ **horseback**, [she won last year's prestigious Kalais races][8]. These are needed skills, for only as a warrior will she earn a citizen's rights. Despite a deep-seated fear **that** she may not be able to kill those blood she shares, she must, [if she's to prove herself to Pell],[9] the fierce warrior she calls father ~~and reveres above all others~~.

To avenge a bloody raid, Pell leads his troops into Daharsha. Thea joins other sixteen-year-olds guarding the border. She's captured by her sire and recognized ~~from~~ **by** her birthmark. **It turns out she** wasn't abandoned, rather returned to A'tal at her ~~captured~~ A'talan mother's request. [Her sire offers his golden stallion as a gift. She doesn't accept, yet throws away her summoner's horn as an excuse for not raising the alarm~~, thus~~ **and** endangering him][10].

[As she gallops back to camp, the golden stallion outstrips Thea's horse. Her horn tied to the stallion's saddle is sufficient betrayal for][11] Pell to cast Thea and the Daharshan horse off the grasslands. Having lost the only family she's ever known and likely a life with the young Venari she hoped to love, she faces a bleak future in Kalais. [As a non-citizen, the whip of A'talan law][12] may result in her arrest, deportation or worse[13]. Seeking Pell's forgiveness, she enters the fall races, [unaware the Mother of All has plans for the child She marked][14].

(A client of this agent) spoke with the online SFF writing group I run. I admire the writers you represent and your outrage at the plight of refugee children suggests DAY WITHOUT DAWN might appeal to you.

I am one of fifteen Society of Master Saddlers Qualified Saddle Fitters in the U.S. My husband and I live on an **eighty-acre**[15] Minnesota farm bordering a wildlife refuge with our herd of Morgan horses. My memberships include RWA and 4th Street Fantasy Society.

The first XYZ pages are pasted below, per your guidelines. Please note that this is a simultaneous submission. I appreciate your time and consideration.

(Signature)

---

1. Great comps. While you can't aim for the crossover market directly (see the feedback chapter for more), it's good to know that the writer is thinking in that direction.
2. Good specificity about series plans here, as well.
3. This sounds nice and dramatic, but I'd be more interested in specifics.
4. This introduces a lot of elements and raises a lot of questions. I'm not sure it's the most fulfilling logline for that reason.
5. This adds a lot of clarity. Consider combining it with the above logline.

6. A subtle grammatical error called the dangling modifier has snuck into this sentence. Learn about it, master it, and try not to do it.
7. By calling her "the child," the writer creates some distance. Instead, focus right in on her, since she's the protagonist.
8. I'd argue this level of detail is unnecessary at the query level.
9. Be clearer about what she wants. Does she care about citizenship? Or is Pell's respect more important? Or does she yearn to make sense of her past? All can be true, but she should have one main driver (at least for the purposes of the query).
10. A lot of detail. This seems *very* subtle and I'm wondering if the writer can summarize instead. For example, "She doesn't accept but doesn't turn him in, either."
11. Same here. Instead, I'd recommend the writer do something simpler, like, "When Pell discovers her betrayal, he casts Thea aside," or similar. Focus on the event, not the details surrounding it.
12. Another dangling modifier.
13. Be specific about stakes!
14. The writer mentions the Mother of All, the Mother Goddess (the same thing?), and Thea's actual mother. Are we talking about two or three entities here?
15. Make sure to hyphenate this.

FICTION QUERY #2 FEEDBACK

WHILE IT'S nice to aim for a "crossover" book (meaning one that appeals to both the YA/children's market and the general fiction market for adult readers), this isn't something that can easily be manufactured unless a publisher commits to publishing (and marketing!) both a children's edition and a general fiction one.

This is discussed in more detail in the Submission Strategy chapter, but this writer should know that a crossover push is unlikely for a debut. More often than not, a book is published as one or the other category, then starts to generate buzz on its own. Once the momentum reaches a certain point and the publisher notices, it repackages the book into another edition, or ramps up another marketing angle. Long story short, a writer can mention that a project has "crossover potential," but this isn't something that writer can really create for themselves.

I do like that the writer is realistic about the series issue. Sure, it *could* stand alone, but it's intended as a series. If that's the way it is, then why hide it? I'm on the fence about category here. On the one hand, this can be pitched as YA due to the character's age. On the other, the word count is high-ish (though fantasy manuscripts can be longer), and the style might appeal to a broad adult fantasy audience. If the initial pitch will be to YA agents and publishers, clarify that in the opening paragraph. This might ultimately come down to voice and writing style.

I'd suggest that the writer try to streamline some of the details. The broad strokes of the plot get a bit lost in all of the logistical description about the horn, for example. This reads a bit like inside baseball to me —important for the plot itself, but not for my understanding of the larger story.

Zoom out a bit and focus on Thea, her desire to belong, her need for Pell's approval, and how she decides to claw her way back to legitimacy. Clarify the issue about the various mother figures/goddesses, too. I got a bit confused here because the Mother Goddess has two names (I think).

Finally, watch out for dangling modifiers. They can be a tricky grammatical error to weed out, but you'll want to avoid them in the query, where the basics count!

FICTION QUERY #3 / LITERARY (235 WORDS)

Dear Agent,

[I am contacting you because you have expressed an interest in literary and historical fiction][1]. This is my first novel. An early version of *Poplar Hill* was a finalist **for** the *Chanticleer Book Reviews* [Chaucer Award for Historical Fiction][2].

[She was cold, she was alone, and she knew she was going to die][3].

In the middle of an epic ice storm, Kitty Stevenson, an eccentric old woman, self-exiled to rural Canada from New York society, [realizes that she is having a heart attack][4]. She had[5] survived Nazi Germany—she *can* survive this, too. Her neighbors mount a heroic effort to save her. [She lives to tell her tale of self-reliance, incredible wealth, poverty, and escape on the eve of a World War][6]. [Kitty is ultimately confronted by what she perceives as a personal moral failure. In the end, she has only one story left to tell: a tale of murder. But, "It was war, damn it, it was war"][7].

Poplar Hill is full of characters reminiscent of E. Annie Proulx's *The Shipping News*, as well as Farley Mowatt's fiction, with a touch of *Tinkers* by Paul Harding.

I have been a general assignment reporter and have five traditionally published trade textbooks, multiple technical columns, and numerous articles to my credit. I currently edit/curate the *Wilderness House Literary Review.*

The entire manuscript is available, fully edited, **at approximately** 78,000 words. **The first XYZ pages are pasted below. Please note that this is a simultaneous submission.** I look forward to hearing from you soon.

Sincerely,

(Signature)

---

1. Careful. This is not actually personalization. This could be said of any agent or publisher who deals in those categories. If the writer's best "personalization" is this kind of "vague-specific" mention, I'd omit it altogether.
2. Make sure to format and cite any prizes or publications correctly. It looks more professional this way. The writer has done this well!
3. A jarring transition. I know the writer wants to start with something grabby, but this is perhaps too gimmicky. It doesn't flow with the rest of the query. It's more of a tease (and almost reads like a manuscript prologue instead of a pitch). Loglines tend to be more specific. I'd omit this and launch right into the following paragraph.
4. This is grabby enough!
5. Awkward tense shift. I'd just say "she survived" because that flows with the rest of the query.
6. Hmm. This sounds like the meat of the narrative is in the past. But the query seems to focus on the present day action. There's a disconnect here, and I wonder which story carries the balance of the novel.
7. This leaves *so many* questions! It's almost better not to mention these elements if the writer won't give the reader more detail. I feel like this is the heart of the story, but I know nothing about it. Certainly not enough to know if I'd like to represent it.

FICTION QUERY #3 FEEDBACK

Some writers on submission absolutely *hate* my advice that they should reveal big plot twists in the query letter (or at the very least, the synopsis). *This is why*. Reading this query, I feel like there's a huge black hole right in the middle of the story. There's a gigantic vulnerability in the character? Great! She is somehow involved in a murder of desperation? Amazing!

But the juiciest details about the novel fall absolutely flat because there's no more context given. A literary agent or publisher will want more data to chew on, simple as that. In addition, it's unclear whether the wartime story is the main narrative or whether the present day carries the book. It seems Kitty's past is much more important to the manuscript, but then why start in the present day? This writer should focus the query along the same lines as the novel itself.

Otherwise, there's a strong bio here, good comps ... I just wish I knew what the heart of this novel was all about. As is, the withholding isn't nearly enough to make me desperate to read.

The query has to give (information) to get (a request).

Conclusion and Resources

CONCLUSION

It's always tough to teach creative writing because there are so many variables. Each creator is unique. So is each idea. The query letter skillset is a bit easier to unpack and codify because it's rather formulaic. But as you can see here, there are forty-three queries, forty-three writers, and forty-three book ideas. Each with their own sensibilities.

As I always tell my editorial clients, you are welcome to "take the wisdom and leave the rest" as you pursue your knowledge of the writing craft. Some of these queries will resonate with you. Others will not. Some of my advice will dovetail with your own instincts. Some will not.

As you read, monitor your own reaction to each letter. Pretend you're a literary agent on the hunt. Which letters do you find the most compelling? Why do you think that might be? Which queries don't work for you (outside of obvious factors like category or genre preference)?

The same goes for the notes. Which advice do you particularly resonate with? Which seems restrictive or unaligned with your approach? Remember, feedback can be very individual and you don't have to swallow everything whole.

Whenever you're faced with writing notes, make sure you consider it with an open mind. But then—if you're sure you haven't let defensiveness or emotional attachment cloud your thinking—you can become more agile at considering feedback, putting the good stuff to use, and letting the rest go.

There's not one way to write a book, nor is there one way to write a query, as the examples in this guide demonstrate. But you can only find *your* way to write a query letter by learning, reading, writing, and trying your best. Then trying again. I cited this Samuel Beckett quote in *Writing Irresistible Kidlit*, and I'll mention it again here because it's *that* good:

"Ever tried. Ever failed.
No matter. Try again.
Fail again. Fail better."

Writing is a lifelong journey, and you are a work in progress. So is your, well, work in progress. Here's to a good story, and a successful submission round.

ARTICLES AND RESOURCES

I've spent over a decade creating educational materials for writers and designing courses, books, and services on writing and publishing topics.

Articles Mentioned In This Book

Throughout this guide, you will notice that I reference some articles over and over again. A few are specific to category, like picture book. I've summarized the most frequently cited articles in the book here (in no particular order):

- "Types of Rejection Letters and Query Rejection": https://kidlit.com/types-of-rejection/
- "How to Write a Novel Synopsis": https://kidlit.com/write-novel-synopsis/
- "How to Write a Query Letter": https://kidlit.com/how-to-write-a-query-letter

- "Query Letter Plot Pitch: Premise vs Plot": https://kidlit.com/plot-pitch/
- "Books That Teach Life Lessons": https://kidlit.com/books-that-teach-life-lessons/
- "Concrete Writing: Using Specific Language": https://kidlit.com/concrete-writing/
- "How to Write Child Characters With Their Own Wisdom": https://kidlit.com/how-to-write-child-characters/
- "Comp Titles in a Query and Other Questions About Book Comps": https://kidlit.com/comp-titles-in-a-query-book-comps/
- "How to Write a Picture Book Query": https://kidlit.com/picture-book-query/
- "Your Query Letter Hook and Revealing the Ending": https://kidlit.com/query-letter-hook
- "Comparative Titles in a Query": https://kidlit.com/comparative-titles/
- "Finding Comp Titles": https://www.goodstorycompany.com/blog/finding-comp-titles/
- "Writing Nonfiction Picture Books": https://kidlit.com/nonfiction-picture-books/
- "Writing a Proactive Protagonist": https://kidlit.com/writing-a-proactive-protagonist/
- "Including Illustration Notes In Your Children's Book Manuscript": https://kidlit.com/childrens-book-manuscript/
- "Submission Tracker Spreadsheet": https://bit.ly/subspreadsheet (Go to "File" and then "Make a copy …" to repurpose it for yourself on your own Google Drive.)

FTC Affiliate Link Disclosure: Some links that appear in this book and point to specific products are affiliate links. I receive affiliate income from Amazon and WritingBlueprints. If you reach these websites and complete a purchase using the links in this resource, I may receive a small commission at no cost to you.

Webinars

I regularly teach free webinars on writing topics like query letters, character, plot, and novel first pages. Some webinars offer the opportunity for live feedback.

Please check out my upcoming Workshops.

I'm also available to Zoom into your critique group or design a presentation or workshop for a writing retreat or conference.

Editorial Services, Ghostwriting, and Writing Workshops

If you enjoyed this book, consider getting personalized one-on-one advice from me. I do query letter editing, of course, but my specialty is deep developmental editing on your entire manuscript. Alternatively, I am happy to step in as a ghostwriter or offer ghost revision for your project. We can also work together in a small group writing workshop intensive setting.

Developmental Editing Services:

marykole.com

Ghost Revision and Ghostwriting Services:

manuscriptstudio.com

Story Mastermind Small Group Writing Workshops:

storymastermind.com

Books and Courses

It is my (perhaps manic) goal to create as many writing resources in as many formats as possible. I hope you find these books and courses useful. I'm always so grateful when a written or recorded version of me can be of service.

***Writing Irresistible Kidlit* Book:**

bit.ly/kolekidlit

Writing Mastery Academy Character Class:

With by Jessica Brody, of *Save the Cat Writes a Novel* fame!

writingmastery.com

Writing Blueprints Submission Resource:

If a deep dive into the submission process sounds helpful, this self-paced course contains over ten hours of instruction. There will definitely be some information overlap between the class and this book, but you'll also get access to agent interviews, over thirty handouts, and a comprehensive step-by-step submission guide.

bit.ly/kolesub

LinkedIn Learning:

linkedin.com/learning/crafting-dynamic-characters

Udemy:

These budget-friendly classes cover assorted writing and publishing topics in an easy-to-digest format.

udemy.com/user/mary-kole

Good Story Company

In 2019, I decided to create Good Story Company as an umbrella brand so that my amazing team and I could collaborate in the service of writing and writers. GSC is where you'll find our most comprehensive library of resources and services.

Good Story Company:

goodstorycompany.com

Good Story Podcast:

goodstorypodcast.com

Good Story YouTube Channel:

youtube.com/goodstory

Good Story Learning Membership:

goodstorycompany.com/membership/

Good Story Marketing:

goodstorycompany.com/marketing

Workshops:

goodstorycompany.com/workshops

WAIT! BEFORE YOU GO!

If you enjoyed this book, there are **three things** you can do to support me and Good Story Company. Thank you so much for your time, kind attention, and consideration!

Subscribe to Our Newsletter!

Our respectful, short, and non-spammy newsletter features all of our latest and greatest free resources, workshops, events, and critique opportunities. Go here to sign up:

https://bit.ly/hellogsc

Leave an Honest Review!

Please also consider leaving a review for this title on your retailer of choice, as well as Goodreads. I love getting feedback of my own, and testimonials help greatly with our discoverability and marketing efforts, so that we can reach more writers.

Reach Out!

Finally, I'd love to hear your experience and celebrate your accomplishments. If you run into some trouble in the writing and publishing worlds, don't be a stranger, either. Drop me a line:

mary@goodstorycompany.com

ACKNOWLEDGMENTS

Thank you to everyone who had supported my work over the years. For this guide, I would be remiss if I didn't express my gratitude to the amazing writers who so graciously gave me permission to use their query letters as teaching examples.

My team at Good Story Company allows me to do the work I love. I'm excited to recognize Kristen Overman, Amy Wilson, Rhiannon Richardson, Michal Leah, Len Cattan-Prugl, Jenna Van Rooy, Kaylee Pereyra, and Kate London.

To all of my marvelous clients and business partners—especially John Cusick and Julie Murphy: I couldn't do what I do without you.

My amazing best friends—Lauren Burris and Scott Marasigan—also win a prize for putting up with me for literal decades. The prize? A lifetime of my nonsense. You're welcome.

Finally, all the love in the world goes to my family. My mother, Liudmila Kondakova, my husband, Todd Macdonald, our kids, Theo, Finn, Ella, and our pets, Gertie, Olive, and Luna: I love you so, so much.

The people listed here are the reason I get up in the morning, and nothing matters more than spending precious time with each and every one of them.

ALSO BY MARY KOLE

Writing Irresistible Kidlit: The Ultimate Guide to Crafting Fiction for Young Adult and Middle Grade Readers

Writing Irresistible Picture Books: Insider Insights Into Crafting Compelling Modern Stories for Young Readers

How to Write a Book Now: Craft Concepts, Mindset Shifts, and Encouragement to Inspire Your Creative Writing

Made in the USA
Monee, IL
13 July 2024

61728910R00160